RACE,
RHETORIC,
and
COMPOSITION

RACE, RHETORIC, and COMPOSITION

Edited by
Keith Gilyard

Series Editor,
Charles I. Schuster

Boynton/Cook Publishers
HEINEMANN
Portsmouth, NH

Boynton/Cook Publishers, Inc.
A subsidiary of Reed Elsevier Inc.
361 Hanover Street
Portsmouth, NH 03801–3912
http://www.boyntoncook.com

Offices and agents throughout the world

Library of Congress Cataloging-in-Publication Data
Race, rhetoric, and composition / edited by Keith Gilyard ; general editor, Charles Schuster.
      p. cm.
      Includes bibliographical references.
      ISBN 0-86709-484-2
      1. English language—Rhetoric—Study and teaching—Social aspects—United States.
      2. English language—Composition and exercises—Social aspects—United States.
      3. Race awareness—United States.   4. United States—Race relations.   I. Gilyard,
Keith, 1952– .   II. Schuster, Charles I.
PE1405.U6R38   1999
808'.042'07—dc21   98-50204
                                                                                                          CIP

Consulting Editor: Charles I. Schuster
Production: Abigail M. Heim
Cover design: Tom Allen, Pear Graphic Design
Manufacturing: Louise Richardson

Printed in the United States of America on acid-free paper
03   02   01   00   99   DA   1   2   3   4   5

To the memory of
George O. Cureton
(1930–1995)

Contents

Preface

Race is discussed nowadays, directly or indirectly, as much as any subject in rhetoric and composition. Any mention in the field of black students, white students, black teachers, or white teachers—and virtually all ruminations about diversity, multiculturalism, or people of color—functions as a racialized speech act inside the nation's racial paradigm. However, much of this talk and its attendant activity has been emotive rather than analytic. In other words, *theorizing race* has yet to catch up with all the personal, albeit necessary, reflections in classrooms and professional outlets. Certainly, given the influence of cultural studies, there has been some movement to inspect race more critically in rhetoric and composition. The aim of this book is to speed things along.

I was inclined initially to demand that contributors to this volume take a hard materialist turn and link race explicitly to historical formations of racism and economic exploitation. The book then would represent a clearly focused rhetorical assault on the idea of race. The unanimous view would be that *race* itself is little more than the language of *race-ism;* the writers would eschew or, at the very least, foreground the labels, categories, and terminologies that constitute and promote "race" dialogue. However, I realized (sensibly so I trust) that this "race thing" is ever shifting, ever changing, and becoming increasingly complex in the ways it marks intellectual and sociopolitical communities. Thus, I changed my platform, seeking instead to publish essays, beyond my own most immediate concerns, that explored various dimensions of race as related to rhetoric and/or composition and at least attempted to render visible the implicit yet dominant discourses on race, racism, and identity.

Malea Powell sets it off, so to speak, by considering what it means to be an "Indian" rhetorician in relation to academe. Drawing on the work of such thinkers as Gerald Vizenor and Wendy Rose—taking exception to some of the ideas of Arnold Krupat—Powell advocates the use of a "mixed-blood/trickster rhetoric" as a means to critique rhetoric and composition and possibly save the field from being another site of academic imperialism.

Through an etymological investigation, Meta Carstarphen explains the source of popular talk about race. She details how concepts of white and black, originally synonymous and not at all used as referents for people, became transmogrified into racialized polar opposites and how fallacies erected on that arrangement still operate in the public sphere. Explicating the *racial enthymeme,* she illustrates the nature of important rhetorical work to be done. Anissa Janine

Wardi, although not as linguistically formal, advances a complementary project. Borrowing Edward Said's notions of "Orientalism" and Roland Barthes'
concept of "mythic signifiers," she demonstrates how "ritualized othering"
helped to account for the wave of anti-Arab sentiment following the 1995 terrorist bombing in Oklahoma City. My own contribution, in line with sentiments
expressed by Carstarphen and Wardi, furthers the call to dismantle racialized
mythology. I briefly historicize "race" and point to some of the baggage sneaked
into composition studies under this rubric.

David G. Holmes identifies parallels between current composition theory
pertinent to African American students and the Black Arts Movement—a controversial stance, but one worth debating. He is concerned that we not *essentialize* African American students by settling for facile notions of identity. Also
highlighting the question of identity, namely her own as a "white" researcher
and teacher, Amy Goodburn examines her own "discursive repertoires and assumptions"—and urges others to do the same—regarding professional writing
about race.

Robert D. Murray, Jr., discusses a rhetorical strategy used by students to
resist certain multicultural pedagogies, a phenomenon he labels "reconstitution." Linking his work primarily to that of Mary Louise Pratt and Richard
Miller, he proffers interventionist strategies for getting students to accept what
he views to be their intellectual responsibilities. Brad Peters, featuring the work
of a female African American student, reveals his attempts to help her develop,
in the context of class and in the face of ethnic and gender bigotry, an enabling
"intersubjective stance." Gail Y. Okawa closes this volume by sharing results
of her work with graduate students grappling with—along with her—issues of
color and race in a course titled "Removing Masks: Exploring American Minority Discourses."

I could have included many more essays if I wished to emphasize expression rather than assessment of opinions regarding the rhetorics *of* race and their
effects. But I would have had almost no essays if I had, in the role of editor, in-
sisted on too strict a materialist slant. What I have angled for, ultimately, is a
modest collection of aligned yet flexibly critical articulations about race, rhetoric, and composition—and, yes, anti-racism—that history, I hope, will prove
worthwhile.

Keith Gilyard

Acknowledgments

In 1995, a few days after the annual meeting of the Conference on College Composition and Communication, on the anniversary of the assassination of Martin Luther King, Jr., I received a call from Charles Schuster. Our conversation boiled down to a simple request on his part: "Do this book." This particular project would not have happened otherwise. I am also grateful to the writers who contributed to this volume and to the staff at Heinemann, especially former editor Peter Stillman. I thank, too, for their invaluable support members of the staff at Syracuse University's Writing Program; namely, George Rhinehart, Marybeth Sorendo, Deborah Saldo, Nance Hahn, and Faith Plvan.

RACE,
RHETORIC,
and
COMPOSITION

1

Blood and Scholarship: One Mixed-Blood's Story[1]

Malea Powell

> It is obvious that there is not a university in this country that is not built on what was once native land. We should reflect on this over and over, and understand this fact as one fundamental point about the relationship of Indians to academia.
>
> Janice Gould
> "The Problem of Being 'Indian':
> One Mixed-Blood's Dilemma"

> Just as a people who oppresses another cannot be free, so a culture that is mistaken about another must be mistaken about itself.
>
> Jean Baudrillard
> *The Mirror of Production*

My grandfather taught me that every good storyteller always acknowledges the place from which her story came—a friend, a gathering, an experience. This story begins not with my own "Indian-ness," but rather with the beginnings of my scholarly interest in the phenomenon of "Indian-ness." As an undergraduate, I took a course on "ethnic and minority women writers of the United States." During the section on "Native Americans," in a journal entry to my instructor, I "confessed" that I was Indian.[2] I did so because some of the ways that the other students had been talking about Native Americans made me uneasy, and I often left class with my stomach churning. My teacher, of course, suggested that I tell the class. I declined. I knew that there was no way that I would live up to my classmates' vision of "authentic Indian"—I wore no feathers or beads, lived in a "normal" house in the middle of an Indiana cornfield, and

1

spoke with the same Midwestern twang as they did. Additionally, the Indians that they constructed through their responses to Leslie Silko's stories and Wendy Rose's and Joy Harjo's poetry were fundamentally different than the Miami, Delaware, Shawnee, Ottawa, Potawatomi, Anishinabe, Lakota, and Cherokee people that I knew. My classmates consistently spoke as if all the "real" Indians had disappeared long ago and all that was left of their culture was stockpiled in the Smithsonian. For them, contemporary Indians were merely sad remnants of a people whose time had passed. So it was here that my project of understanding and articulating American Indian rhetorics began.

What follows is a series of stories. There is a story about how the narratives that shape "America" and the "Academy" also shape what it can mean to be "Indian" and what it can mean to be an "Indian scholar." There is a story about blood and seeing, and a speculative story about mixed-blood/trickster rhetoric. None of these are *separate* stories—they are all interdependent, all intertwined, all related. I tell these stories partially—I tell them as I hear them, and I recognize that my act of listening does not, cannot tell the *whole* story, nor would I want it to. These tellings, then, are part of a *listening game,* in the Lyotardian sense, "in which the important thing is to listen, . . . And in this game, one speaks only inasmuch as one listens; that is, one speaks as a listener, and not as an author" (Lyotard and Thebaud 1985, 71–72). I listen for unheard stories, counter-stories, which are usually silenced by the narratives that construct "life" in these United States.[3] In telling these stories, I am attempting to ask Victor Villanueva's question from "Rhetoric Is Politics"; that is, "How do nice people abide by and maintain not nice things, like a system in which certain groups are consistently relegated to the bottom of the structure in disproportionate numbers?" (1994, 332). I believe that taking Villanueva's question seriously is part of following Beverly Moss' advice to "take stock of where we [the discipline of rhetoric and composition] have come from, where we are, and where we think we are headed—especially before we get there" (1993, 347).

In positioning myself as a scholar who does American Indian rhetorics, I want consciously to mark both portions of that figuration. The *rhetoric* part emerges from Jim Berlin's "social epistemic rhetoric" (107) in that it attempts to mediate and negotiate the material contradictions of multiply positioned and constructed subjects; the *American Indian* part is linked to my often perplexing experience as a mixed-blood. In this double-marking, I hope to initiate a mixed-blood methodology,[4] one that mixes postcolonial theory with powwow observations, imperial agendas with indigenous resistance. To do so is to enact what Gerald Vizenor[5] calls *survivance*—a pose I interpret as survival plus resistance—and to call for the entrance of the trickster[6] who lives in counter-stories (1994, 4). This mixed-blood pose is important because, as Jana Sequoya describes it, we (i.e., Indian scholars) are involved in a "contest of stories," whose outcome will determine "the issue of viable material conditions for sustaining Indian identity" (1993, 469). As a scholar[7] who is also an Indian, as a participant in this struggle, I am suspicious of my own imbrication, my own complicity, within the Academy,[8] an institution predicated on Western European ideas and values. Though I have questioned my own implicatedness at every stage of this project, I suspect that, in the end, I have not been suspicious enough. Additionally, I am obliged to tell a story that respects and aids the people whose voices and spirits construct a larger web of existence for me than ever can (or should) be explained in "scholarly" discourse. These stories that I tell are ones that I am not able to escape or ignore.

To begin this survivance story, I want to take up the question of what happens when we study Indians *in any way* within the Academy. In other words, what happens when we delve into that cacophony of narratives that shapes our scholarly understanding of "Indians?" We must recognize, as well, that the narratives of *Indian* and *Academy* are always already a part of an even larger story—the narrative that constructs America[9] and American-ness.[10] After all, it is because of how America—the ideological state and collective national culture—came into being that there is an "American" scholarly experience and a specific scholarly discourse about Native Americans at all. The stories that write this "American" narrative are familiar ones—"Christopher Columbus and the Discovery," "Pioneers and Manifest Destiny." Our familiarity with this "American" story is precisely the point here in relation to Indian peoples. Jimmie Durham, Cherokee poet/artist and American Indian Movement activist, claims that "America's narrative about itself centers upon a hidden text concerning its relationship with American Indians" (1992, 425).

A central component of this "American tale" is the settlers' vision of the frontier, a frontier that is "wilderness," empty of all "civilized" life. The settler is a brave individual who sets forth to pit *his* (and I use the male pronoun here deliberately) skills of "civilization" against this vast wilderness; *he* tames the wilderness, domesticates it, and installs in it the icons of civilization—Euro-American town life, commerce, roads, railroads, churches, stores, and schools. The un-seeing of Indian peoples, nations, and civilizations is obvious here. For the colonizers, it is a necessary un-seeing; material Indian "bodies" are simply not seen so that the mutilations, rapes, and murders that characterized this first-wave genocide also simply are not seen. "Un-seeing" Indians gave (and still give) Euro-Americans a critical distance from materiality and responsibility, a displacement that is culturally valued and marked as "objectivity." What is not so obvious is the correspondence of this frontier story to the stories that construct the Academy and its scholarly practices.

The "rules" of scholarly discourse—the legitimizing discourse of the discipline of rhetoric and composition—require us to write ourselves into this frontier story. Scholars are to set forth on the fringes of "the known" in order to stake out and define a piece of "unoccupied" scholarly territory that, through our skill at explicating and analyzing, will become our own scholarly homestead, our area of concentration. We are trained to identify our object of study in terms of its boundaries, its difference from other objects of study, and then to do everything within our power to bring that object into the realm of other "known" objects. In effect, we "civilize" unruly topics. And it is our distance from those topics, the fact of our displacement from the materiality of these areas of study, that lends legitimacy to our efforts. We must be objective scholars, fair in our assessments, detailed in our descriptions, and unfailingly unemotional if our work is to be taken seriously.

This scholarly homestead-plot is our price of admission into the Academy. However, these "rules," when applied to the study of indigenous peoples, end up producing what I call second-wave genocide. Not only does the imperial power commit material acts meant to crush an unruly indigenous population, but also its institutions of intellectual and cultural exchange (i.e., universities) make the rules by which the first-wave genocide will be studied, and these same rules apply to the study of genocide survivors. Indians can be studied only within the terms of the oppressor; the Academy becomes just another powerful agent of imperialism.

I don't mean to disable scholarly work here. On the contrary, I want to remind us all of the depth and breadth of the contaminated-ness of the so-called "tools" with which we go about our daily work. In his introduction to *Black Athena,* Martin Bernal reminds us that, while we ourselves may no longer be explicitly racist, we are often "still working with models set up by men who were crudely . . . racist" (1987, 9). Like Bernal, I don't believe that any scholarly work can be fully enabled until we see the entire web of narratives in which it exists and works to create meaning. We cannot separate scholarship in the United States from the "American tale." We cannot separate the material exterminations of first-wave genocide in North America (beginning in 1492) from the intellectual and cultural exterminations of second-wave genocide, a process that has been ongoing since the Indian Removal Act of 1830.[11] But we can begin, by consciously and explicitly positioning our work within this distasteful collection of narratives, to open space for the existing stories that might run counter to the imperial desires of traditional scholarship, stories that have been silenced by its hegemonic drone.

On Madison Avenue, the recognition factor of the "Indian" image "outranks, on a world scale, that of Santa Claus, Mickey Mouse, and Coca Cola combined" (Dorris 1987, 99). It is the very centrality of this image that complicates any scholarly work on Indian peoples. We are all, Indian and non-Indian alike, inscribed—written—by these narrative images. They tell a story that we have heard so loudly for so long that we have become numb to their presence.[12] Scholars who concentrate on the study of Native American culture, history, and literature often, even as they attempt to disrupt this master narrative, create a kind of sympathetic echo behind it: a sort of popular scholarly narrative that is characterized by outrage and concern about the lack of Native American voices. Its resolution is twofold: a collective effort to *re-create* those voices, speaking for Native Americans directly or as an "authorizing" force for those voices, and as an effort to *penetrate* and thereby legitimate the counter-stories, seeing them as explicable objects of study. This need to control and legitimate (in scholarly terms) counter-stories is glaring in Arnold Krupat's introduction to the Smithsonian-sponsored anthology *New Voices in Native American Literary Criticism.* Krupat[13] writes:

> I believe it is the case that in recent years some academic researchers have wanted very much to take seriously, even, indeed, to base their research upon not only Native experience but Native constructions of the category of knowledge. Still, as I have said, the question remains: *How to do so?* It is an urgent question, inasmuch as a good number of us are quite clear that we do not wish to "domesticate the savage mind," or to engage in imperial acts of translation that simply override indigenous experiential and conceptual understandings. But, if, nonetheless, *we are still unwilling to abandon some commitment to the scientific perspective* as more than just the Western worldview universalized, we encounter problems that cannot simply be undone by good intentions. And, for now, such a perspective, while it must of course take into account "the reality" of . . . Native American "existence" as native people "experience it," it *still cannot, I think, base its explanations/interpretations on that experiential reality.* (1993, xix–xx, emphasis mine)

When scholars convince themselves that they cannot study Indians (i.e., others) from the basis of Indian experience and existence, that they must make their efforts "scientific" and thus distance their work from Indian "reality," they displace the very voices—those of Indian peoples—that they claim they want to hear. They convince themselves that they are no longer influenced by those imperial American narratives, those media (and mediated) images of "Indianness," and that *their* work can be "scientific." To assume that an admiration for Native American culture coupled with a position within the Academy will somehow offer protection from the "smarminess" of American cultural imperialism is to open up room for Indian cultures to be appropriated, distorted, and objectified in increasingly new and approved "scholarly" terms.

In the United States, the scholarly legitimation narrative is predicated on a notion that "precludes those of that [Euro-derived] tradition from acknowledging either the fact or meaning of their own ethnicity" (Rose 1992, 410). It is this sublimation of ethnicity that leads to a kind of "we're all the same inside" mentality that ultimately shuts down and erases difference. Materially, the imperial policies of the United States have erased, consumed, and imprisoned the "differences" of Indian peoples; now the Academy mirrors these policies by imprisoning indigenous experiences in a Euro-centered intellectual frame. As Hopi/Miwok poet and theorist Wendy Rose points out, "the inclusion of non-European intellectual content in the academy is absolutely predicated upon its conformity to sets of 'standards' conceived and administered by those adhering to the basic precepts of Euro-derivation" (1992, 407). Not only are Indians marginalized and "erased" as objects of study, the Indian scholar is often marginalized and overwritten by the rules of the Academy:

> The basic "qualification" demanded by academe of those who would teach non-European content [and for those of non-European origin] is that they first

receive "advanced training" and "socialization" in doctoral programs steeped in the supposed universality of Euro-derivation. (1902, 407)

Native knowledge is eschewed for many American Indian scholars who must "prove" themselves on a frontier already "settled" and "civilized." As Dorris points out, the "conviction that the West holds a virtual monopoly on 'science,' logic, and clear-thinking" writes a specific narrative for the Indian scholar who studies some aspect of Indian culture (1987, 102), one in which said scholar is marked as "hopelessly subjective and biased, and much of their work is dismissed as self-serving" (104). This attitude toward Indian scholars is particularly odd in that "Euro-Americans have not felt shy in writing about their respective ancestors and are not automatically accused of aggrandizing them" (104).

Imagine this:

You are standing in a room. The walls of this room are covered in blood. All around you are corpses of varying vintage. They are bloody and putrid; they stink and their spirits howl. You must pick your way over these corpses as you go about your business in that room, whatever that may be, but there is no way to avoid them, no way to shut them out of your consciousness, no way to stop hearing and seeing and breathing their existence. Now imagine that in this room are other people—like you, but not quite like you—you see, they can't see or smell or hear these dead bodies. You keep telling them to be careful, not to step here or there. You keep asking, "Don't you see anything here? Don't you hear anything?" They smile and say, "Of course not, what's to see or hear?" They begin to think that you are crazy and maybe you begin to think so too. Worse yet, some of these people are willing to admit that you might just be seeing and hearing things that they cannot, or will not, allow themselves to see or hear, but that you should quit calling attention to yourself, that you should shut up, at least until you accrue enough power that people will listen to you—and that the only way for you to get any power is if you pretend that you aren't seeing what you are seeing, hearing what you are hearing. "Act like everybody else," they tell you. "Go along with the rules."

I want to move, now, to another story, this time one that is told by a Euro-American scholar who focuses his theoretical and critical work on American Indians. I offer this story as an example of the utter ease with which counter-stories are unseen and, ultimately, unheard by even the most well-intentioned scholar. At one point early in *Ethnocriticism,* Krupat tells a story that is meant to illustrate how completely ineffective "postmodernism" is as a material po-litical strategy.[14] It is a revealing story, so I will quote it at length:

As I have worked on this book over the past two years, I have many times taken a break by looking out the window, at Tomkins Square park. From per-haps the summer of 1989 until their removal on December 13, 1989, there were a great many speakers to be seen and heard in the park. Mostly black and

Hispanic, mostly homeless, some down on their luck, some severely disturbed, or badly addicted, the park people audibly told stories to each other; to the working class cops who, for a while, at least, were gathered here thicker than thieves; to the Yuppies who, hurrying to their new renovations, didn't stop to listen. Until the 1988 police riot, the homeless most thickly congregated at the south end of the park, at Seventh Street; after, most of them moved their tarpaulin, box, and board shelters over to Tenth Street, the north end of the park, where I lived. The population density of the park people increased as the summer of 1989 ended. . . . Walking in the park (it is quite safe by day), having Rorty and Lyotard and Carroll in mind, I tried to listen to the stories being told; I tried, too, to see these *petits récits,* the *wisps of narrative* unquestionably produced by the people in the park as "dissident" in some meaningful way, a "challenge to the dominant metanarrative or state apparatus that would prohibit or discredit them." But it is their marginality and complete containment that most strike me. . . . (1992, 11–12)

Consider, for a moment, the position of Krupat in this story. He is a relentless observer, looking at "these" people first from his window and then as he walks among them, seeming to listen. From this story, we would have to gather that he never attempted to either talk to or interact with any of his subjects in any way—he only watched—a monologic positioning. Within this story, he recites how hard he tried to see their discourse as "'dissident' in some meaningful way." Meaningful for whom—the speakers in the park, their dialogic listeners, himself (their monologic listener), New York City, New York State, the United States, the world, the Academy? His dismissal of their discourse, of their speech, as meaningless *because* of its marginality and seeming "containment" reveals much more about the scholar than it does about this discourse he is positing as "postmodernism."

What about this storytelling event? Significantly, Krupat chooses to tell a story in the midst of his argument against postmodernism. He's contributing his own *petite récit,* his own narrative wisp here, and he tries to use his story to subvert the credibility, the sense-ability, of his construction of postmodernism. It seems ironic that in order to subvert a narrative about how stories are subversive, he feels pressed to offer a subversive story himself. What Krupat leaves out of his story is revealing: He leaves out the voices of the people in the park. What were they saying? He just tells us *about* them, looks *at* them, a flaw that he readily acknowledges in most "traditional Western disciplinary theory and practice as these have operated in relation to Native American subjects in all senses of that word" (1992, 7), but a flaw that he doesn't seem willing, or able, to acknowledge as present in his own construction of these park people, these marginal others.

The precise effects of these speakers in this park, of their narrative wisps (i.e., counter-stories), and of other speakers in other parks, other places, can't be seen immediately, but to deny that they have *any* effect simply because they do not have an immediate and far-reaching effect that is visible to him seems ridiculous. Krupat introduces this story with a challenge to postmodernism à la Jean-François Lyotard and David Carroll. He writes, "I would challenge them to name *specifically* not even 'hundreds, [or] thousands of [the] little dissident narratives they have in mind but even a couple of dozen that have had any social effectivity whatsoever" (1992, 11). If his "gripe" with postmodernism is that it is not an effective strategy for political change, then how does he characterize the material, political change that his own work "should" be doing? Beyond the walls of the Academy, who listens to Krupat's stories?

Krupat follows his "people in the park" story with an entreaty to engage in something more than a privileged language game, but never considers the privileged position of his own discourse.[15] In *Ethnocriticism*, he is trying to construct a "rather less violent" (6) way to do Native studies:

> An adequate ethnocriticism for Native American culture, history, and literature, so far as it may be established at all . . . will only be achieved by a means of complex interactions between a variety of Western discursive and analytic modes and a variety of non-Western modes of knowing and understanding. The Western modes are quite well known, and I continue to think that, in spite of some inevitable distortions, they are still, at least in some measure, useful for an encounter with native American literary materials. . . . Native modes of knowing and understanding are not well known, and that is in large measure because they have not been formulated as analytic or critical modes apart from the verbal performance they would know and understand. (1992, 43–44)

What is missing here in this call for assimilation is an interrogation of who is directing this integration of Western and Native epistemology—the simple acknowledgment of who will do the "civilizing" and "expanding" to whom.

It would seem that an Indian scholar is in an impossible bind. Limited by the master narratives constructing her, the stories she can tell *that will be heard* are limited. What I am suggesting is that there are some stories that can be told and heard, like this story that I am telling, revelatory stories that open space for counter-stories and resistance, mixed-blood stories told from the borders of Indian-ness, American-ness, Scholarly-ness. Joseph Bruchac suggests that we think of the position of mixed-bloods as a kind of *metis* story, and he does so for a very particular reason. *Metis* is a Lakota word (derived from the French *métis* for *cross-breed* or *hybrid*) that "refers to a person of mixed blood," but it translates literally into English as "translator's son." "It means that you are able to understand the language of both sides, to help them understand each other" (Bruchac 1993, 244–245). Gloria Anzaldúa calls this "a consciousness of the Borderlands," the domain of the *mestiza* (1987, 77). In Anzaldúa's configuration, the *mestiza* is presented with a sea of possibilities, "conflicting information and points of view" (79). The only way for the mixed-blood to survive is by "developing a tolerance for contradictions, a tolerance for ambiguity," and by turning those contradictions and ambiguities into "something else" (79).

Anishinabe writer and theorist Gerald Vizenor would have Indian scholars/ mixed-bloods play trickster, to use our knowledge of the language and structure that compose the narratives that bind us as instruments to cut away those same oppressive stories.

Vizenor celebrates the humor and play room that are made available to *crossbloods*[16] (what I've been calling mixed-bloods) in the simultaneity of our positions on the margins of American culture combined with our iconographic centrality against which much "American-ness" is imagined. Sharp humor (yes, sharp like a weapon) and radical temporal figurings (we are always at the past and the future in the present, and vice versa) help Vizenor to posit the trickster as a space of liberation. He does so in *Narrative Chance* by textually refusing to participate in his own remaking. He will not become an "absolute fake," a Native American constructed only for scholarly consumption (1989, 5). Instead, he invites us—the "participant audience" (196)—into a game of narrative chance, where meanings are pressed together from the very narrative wisps that Krupat discards. Vizenor would not disregard or discard the discourse of Krupat's "park people." To the contrary, he would cite Krupat's disregard for their marginal narratives as *proof* of their subversive potential and of their political importance. The "park people" toss their words about like dice in a game of narrative chance. To listen and to hear them would make us participants; their words would be counter-stories, running against the current of Krupat's disdain.

For me, the trickster is central to imagining a "mixed-blood rhetoric." The trickster is many things, and is no thing as well. Ambivalent, androgynous,[17] anti-definitional, the trickster is slippery and constantly mutable. Vizenor finds the trickster everywhere, but particularly at work in communal "tribal" discourse.[18] I find the trickster in every nook and cranny of daily life as a mixed-blood. But, more important, I see the trickster at work outside of Indian-ness as well, in the contrarinesses that inhabit the stories that tell, and un-tell, America and the Academy. The trickster isn't really a person, it is a "communal sign," a "concordance of narrative voices" (1989, 12) that inhabits the "wild space over and between sounds, words, sentences, and narratives" (196). Trickster discourse does "play tricks," but they aren't malicious tricks, not the hurtful pranks of an angry child; instead, the tricks reveal the deep irony that is always present in whatever way we choose to construct reality. Trickster discourse is deflative; it exposes the lies we tell ourselves and, at the same time, exposes the necessity of those lies to our daily material existence. Trickster discourse asks "Isn't the world a crock of shit?," but also answers with "Well, if we didn't have this crock of shit, what would we do for a world?" The trickster asks us to be fully conscious to the simple inconsistencies that inhabit our reality.

The version of trickster, or mixed-blood, rhetoric that I am offering here is not so much opposed to modernity or social science or postmodernity or frontiers or to business as usual within the discipline of rhetoric and composition as it is *related* to them—a very different configuration in which it is the rhetor's very *relationship with* oppressive discourses that opens a space of possibility.

Practicing this kind of relational mixed-blood rhetoric, then, means following the Academy's, the discipline's, "rules" by transgressing them, not just to oppose them but to transform them, to change utterly the grounds upon which our scholarship exists. This rhetoric, then, takes a kind of cross-blood understanding and materiality, a form of mixed-blood movement in theoretical space, that the Academy's legitimizing narrative is slow to acknowledge and value. Such a rhetoric is based on relationality and movement across cultural/institutional boundaries, and presupposes that those who enact it have an experiential understanding of the cultures/institutions that they propose to transverse.

Recently, some intellectual friends of mine and I have tried to enact a sort of trickster rhetoric within our own scholarly practices. Because the trickster is "real in those who imagine the narrative" (Vizenor 1989, 190), we are trying to imagine ourselves differently as scholars. Allied as the Crossblood Collective, we have begun with transgressions—counter-stories—that may appear, like those of Krupat's park people, to have little or no immediate effect. For example, take the formality of conference "rules" like those of the Conference on College Composition and Communication (CCCC) that require proposal submissions to "fit" into particular group configurations—panels, roundtables, and forums—which seriously limit the possibilities for collective (not just collaborative) scholarship. The way to get around these rules, of course, is to lie—to propose a "panel," for example, and to submit the requisite number of abstracts and individual names with the explicit intent of turning the "position paper" format of a "panel" into a collectively delivered paper. This is just one small way that, as a collective, we try to put our politics into practice. It is our relationship to the CCCC that makes such transgressions possible, but it is our alliance as mixed-blood scholars that makes it necessary.

In many ways, this rhetoric, these trickster turns, has already been enacted by nineteenth-century Indian intellectuals like Sarah Winnemucca Hopkins[19] and Charles Alexander Eastman,[20] who simultaneously enacted compliance with and resistance to Euro-American culture in their written and oral texts. In doing so, they enacted a sort of "tactical authenticity," a move that established themselves as "real" Indians within the discourses of their historical moment and then used that "real-ness" as a space of privilege and possibility from which they could deliver a critique of Euro-American culture. In many ways these trickster stories have never stopped being told—around the dance circle, the campfire, at the powwow—have never stopped being listened to and heard by those of us who see and hear and live within tribal stories, the space that opens in a poem or short story or novel when the contradictory-ness of "Indian" is revealed and embraced. Some of us, after all, can't help but see the bodies, the blood, as we stand in that room . . . listening . . . hearing.

These stories, in large part, have all been leading up to this: I am at war[21] with my rhetoric relations. Wendy Rose, in her poetry volume *Going to War with All My Relations,* explains that this is "a special kind of war—one in

which struggle is honorable and just, but also one in which there are no muti-
lated soldiers or plundered villages" (1993, vii). This is not a war that requires
a victor, but one in which my participation, through honorable struggle, is necessary. I believe that rhetoric as a discipline has been and continues to be com-
plicit with the imperial project of scholarship in the United States. I believe that
rhetoric as a discipline does not see the foundation of blood and bodies upon
which it constitutes itself. I believe that many of us who work within this discipline participate daily in un-seeing, in denying, and, in doing so, perpetuate
the myth of the empty continent. I believe that scholarship in America can
never be staked forth on neutral ground. I believe that even as the marginalized
and radical "anti-disciplinary" and/or "cross-disciplinary" discipline, rhetoric
takes for granted its originary relation to Greece and Europe—its fundamental
relationship to imperialism—and gives little critical thought at all to the geographical space in which it now exists. I believe that rhetoric, as a discipline
and as it is enacted by its scholars/teachers, merely tolerates "other" discourses
at its margins. It does not take into account, for example, work on African
American or American Indian discourse strategies as it constitutes itself as a
"theoretical" discipline with the help of Foucault, Lyotard, Nietzche, Kristeva,
Cixous, et cetera. These "marginal" groups make no impact on the important
project of gaining Academic power for the discipline, but are pointed to constantly as "proof" of the discipline's inclusiveness.

Those who doubt the existence of these "tolerated margins" need only look
again at the 1997 "Call for Proposals" for the CCCC and see that the possible categories of submission—the "area clusters"—clearly separate histories
(Area Cluster 103) and theories (Area Cluster 102) of rhetoric from "writing in
a global context" (Area Cluster 108) and from "writing and difference" (Area
Cluster 107) and from methodology (Area Cluster 109) and pedagogy (Area
Cluster 101). The ghetto-ization present in the area clusters is rationalized
as "practical," a way to apportion the large number of incoming proposals to
"knowledgeable" reviewers. However, in praxis, these categories also are used
to "group" items on the program so that it's possible to go to every section
generically marked "methodology," for example, and never encounter a session in which issues of difference are being taken up by scholars of color. This
"tolerated-margins" approach to dividing up disciplinary knowledge must
change if the discipline of rhetoric and composition is ever to become more
than just another site of Academic imperialism.

My final story, then, is a call for a reimagining of this disciplinary space
that is conscious of, and conscionable in relation to, the ideological position of
the Academy within this continent—a reimagining that listens carefully to
those bloody, invisible bodies—and not just to the bodies of American Indians,
but also to the bodies of the African slaves and the Asian laborers, as well as to
the bodies of their contemporary relations who continue to resist the advances
of imperialism today. This reimagining doesn't always celebrate itself (as rhetoric and composition studies have been inclined to do in recent years) because

it recognizes that its celebratory status comes at the expense of other bodies, other ways of knowing. Because I am a rhetorician, I hope that these stories have been persuasive or at least provocative. Because I am an Indian, I hope these stories have urged you to listen and to hear. But because I am a mixed-blood, I am willing to accept that neither may have occurred, and that I will have to try again. The abiding quality of mixed-blood rhetoric is its persistence and patience, as well as its ambiguity and contradictions.

Notes, or Other Stories

1. This essay is dedicated to my mother, Nan Meiring, and to my daughter, Audrey Swartz, who are my immediate links in this spiral of life. I am deeply indebted to Michael Wojcik for his nurturing companionship, to my good friends Jill Swiencicki and Dominic Micer for their careful readings and productive commentary on earlier drafts of this essay, and to the members of the Crossblood Collective—Janice Gould, Scott Lyons, Ellen Cushman, and Terese Monberg for their generous intellectual and emotional support. Our collective discussions about *mestiza*/mixed-blood consciousness and methodology, dissent, war, resistance, and ghosts have enlivened and enriched any work that I will ever do, either as a member of the Collective or as an "individual" scholar. Although this essay was begun before this collective was constituted, it nevertheless bears more than the traces of all our voices and struggles.

2. I identify myself as an Eastern Miami, Shawnee, Welsh mixed-blood.

3. These imperial narratives are, of course, intimately connected with the construction of "race" as a category of imposed identity and as a theoretical trope for othering that not only allows, but also ensures, hierarchical privileging of some "races" (Anglo and Euro-American) over others. For a more detailed discussion of this, see Frantz Fanon's *Black Skin, White Masks* (New York: Grove Weidenfeld, 1967, trans. Markmann) and Homi Bhabha's "The Other Question: The Stereotype and Colonial Discourse" (from *The Sexual Subject,* New York: Routledge, 1992, 312–331).

4. I want to be very specific about how I'm using the term *mixed-blood.* Among many Indian peoples, a mixed-blood is literally a person whose blood-quantum is mixed, usually Indian and Euro-American. Mixed-bloods are sometimes seen as tainted, neither an "Indian" nor a "White." Because of acculturation and assimilation, many Indians are legally mixed-bloods. I don't use *mixed-blood* literally to refer to U.S.-government–enforced "pedigree." I use *mixed-blood* as a figurative description for a person who "lives" between cultures that are epistemologically contradictory and that experience asymmetrical power relations. The particular example from which this text arises is that of an American Indian person who has been exposed—to one degree or another—to the culture of her particular nation as well as to the dominant (i.e., Euro-American) culture in this country. I use *mixed-blood* subversively, then, to designate a particular construction of subjectivity and as a reminder of how dominant cultural narratives "value" American Indian peoples according to their "pedigree." For more information about legal definitions of "Indian," see M. Annette Jaimes' "Federal Indian Identification Policy" (*The State of Native America: Genocide, Colonization, and Resistance,* M. Annette Jaimes, ed. Boston: South End Press, 1992) and Joyotpaul Chaudhuri's "American Indian Policy" (*American Indian Policy in the Twentieth Century,* Vine Deloria, Jr., ed. Norman, OK: University of Oklahoma Press, 1992).

5. Gerald Vizenor is a mixed-blood Anishinabe critical theorist and writer who is known for scholarship that combines postmodern theory with "tribal" consciousness and for his trickster novels and short stories. His works include *Manifest Manners: Postindian Warriors of Survivance* (1994); *Crossbloods: Bone Courts, Bingo, and Other Reports* (1990); *Narrative Chance: Postmodern Discourse on Native American Indian Literatures* (1989); *The Trickster of Liberty: Tribal Heirs to a Wild Baronage* (1988); and *Griever: An American Monkey King in China* (1990; winner of the American Book Award).

6. The trickster is a common figure in many American Indian cultures and is often underestimated by anthropologists as *only* a character in oral stories. The trickster I elaborate upon in this essay is similar to the African American signifying practices described by H.L. Gates in *The Signifying Monkey: A Theory of Afro American Literary Criticism* (New York: Oxford University Press, 1988) and relies heavily on articulations by Gerald Vizenor in "Socioacupuncture: Mythic Reversals and the Striptease in Four Scenes" (*The American Indian and The Problem of History,* Calvin Martin, ed., New York: Oxford University Press, 1987) and *Narrative Chance.* For conventional readings of the trickster, see Paul Radin's *The Trickster: A Study in American Indian Mythology* (New York: Schocken, 1956). For more playful readings (besides Vizenor's), see Ward Churchill's *Indians Are Us?* (Monroe: Common Courage, 1994) and *Fantasies of the Master Race* (Monroe: Common Courage, 1992), and indigenous writers like Beth Brant, Janice Gould, Wendy Rose, Joy Harjo, and Chrystos and Kimberly Blaeser.

7. For the purpose of this study, I am assuming that a *scholar* is someone who "challenges or problematizes traditional assumptions and theories" (Sullivan 1992, 41).

8. By *Academy* I mean that site of institutionalized intellectual activity that is imagined to take place in the colleges and universities of the United States.

9. I use *America* in the imprecise ideological sense of that entity geographically located in North America that calls itself The United States of America. For a fuller discourse on "America," see Benedict Andersen's *Imagined Communities* (London: Verso, 1983) and Jack D. Forbes' "What Do We Mean By America and American" (*News from Indian Country,* VIII.12, 1994, 16–17).

10. Again, imprecisely, I use *American-ness* to identify a sort of cultural ethos, founded in Western European values and belief systems, that is associated with the United States of America. This collective culture values all things European over all things indigenous, and is that sense of "patriotism" invoked in songs like "America the Beautiful" or "My Country 'Tis of Thee"; this ethos is strongly connected to the United States' imperial identity.

11. The Indian Removal Act of 1830 was one of the first instances in which "friends" of the Indian joined forces with land speculators. The Act was signed by President Andrew Jackson and reserved land west of the Mississippi, erroneously called the "Great American Desert," for Indian settlement. Eastern Indian nations, like the Cherokee, were "relocated" by the federal government to the West, primarily to Oklahoma and Kansas (*Native Americans in the Twentieth Century,* James S. Olson and Raymond Wilson, Urbana, IL: University of Illinois Press, 1986).

12. I take this from Wendy Rose's "Backlash" (*The Halfbreed Chronicles,* Minneapolis: West End, 1985). "It's not that your songs / are so much stronger / or your feet more deeply / rooted, but that / there are many of you / shouting in a single voice / like a giant child" (38).

13. Krupat is an influential Euro-American scholar in American Indian Studies. His works include *Ethnocriticism: Ethnography, History, Literature* (1992); *The Voice in the Margin* (1989); *Recovering the Word* (with Brian Swann, 1987); and *For Those Who Come After* (1985).

14. Krupat's configuration of "postmodernism" is based on his readings of Lyotard from *The Postmodern Condition: A Report on Knowledge* (Minneapolis: University of Minnesota Press, 1984) and of Carroll from "Narrative, Heterogeneity, and the Question of the Political: Bakhtin and Lyotard" in *The Aims of Representation* (New York: Columbia University Press, 1987).

15. While this is a problematic predicament, it is not unnegotiable. Krupat and other Euro-American scholars could explicitly admit their privileged positions as part of their scholarship and could use the privilege they've gained to help the people that their scholarship often objectifies. Vine Deloria, Jr., has proposed such a reciprocal relationship (see "Research, Redskins, and Reality," *American Indian Quarterly,* Fall 1991, 457–468). This, of course, would require that they be critical of their characterizations of Indian peoples as well. In the long quote that follows this note in my text, Krupat alludes that Native "modes of knowing" aren't widely known or understood because Native peoples can only articulate their ways of knowing in verbal performance, not in the "analytic or critical" modes of the Academy. This simply does not correspond to the material presence of long-time scholars like Vine Deloria, Jr., and Simon Ortiz, nor does it acknowledge contemporary Indian scholarship.

16. *Crossbloods* are, according to Vizenor, "the agonistic survivors" of imperialism, "a postmodern tribal bloodline, an encounter with racialism, colonial duplicities, sentimental monogenism, and generic cultures"; "crossbloods are communal, and their stories are splendid considerations of survivance" (1990, vii–viii).

17. Gender is a category that goes unanalyzed due to the scope of this essay. However, the androgyny of the trickster offers compelling possibilities for unpacking gender binaries in feminist rhetorics. In stories, the trickster is often assigned gender, but frequently cross-dresses and mutates as well. Highly sexualized in many stories, the trickster is an "erotic shimmer in oral traditions" (Vizenor 1989, 188).

18. Although I find the word *tribal* problematic in the ways it has been used by the U.S. government as a way to construct Indian peoples as "uncivilized," thus rationalizing colonial policies, Vizenor embraces the term as a way to "avoid the traps, the historical traps" implied by the word *Indian* (from *Survival This Way: Interviews with American Indian Poets,* Joseph Bruchac, Sun Tracks and University of Arizona Press, 1987). One of the pleasures of the Indian community in this country is the awareness of how words work to construct meaning, and how that meaning plays off of stereotypes and images. Implicit in that awareness is that colonized people should name themselves, and should feel comfortable with those names. Although I choose a different name to embrace, *Indian,* I understand Vizenor's distaste for it as well.

19. Sarah Winnemucca Hopkins, a Paiute, was a popular speaker on behalf of Indian rights during the late nineteenth century. She fought for her people's right to live on their Humboldt River lands for most of her life and gained a powerful audience—Boston activist Elizabeth Peabody and Senator Henry Dawes. Winnemucca's speeches were said to help bring about passage of the Dawes (Allotment) Act. She published one book, *Life Among the Piutes: Their Wrongs and Claims* in 1891, shortly before her

death. For more information, see Katherine Gehm's *Sarah Winnemucca: Most Extraordinary Woman of the Paiute Nation* (Phoenix: O'Sullivan, Woodside & Co., 1975).

20. Charles Alexander Eastman, a Santee Sioux (Dakota), lived during the late nineteenth and early twentieth centuries. Born on the reservation and educated in Euro-American schools (i.e., Beloit College Preparatory School, Knox College Preparatory School, Kimball Union Academy, Dartmouth College, and Boston University Medical School), Eastman became a doctor and was the agency physician at Pine Ridge during the massacre of Wounded Knee in 1890. Eastman became an activist and wrote several books, most notably *From the Deep Woods to Civilization* (Boston: Little, Brown, 1916) and *The Soul of the Indian* (New York: Houghton Mifflin, 1911). For more information on Eastman, see Raymond Wilson's *Ohiyesa, Charles Eastman, Santee Sioux* (Urbana, IL: University of Illinois Press, 1983).

21. I use the word *war* here deliberately, not to construct the position of mixed-bloods, or mixed-blood methodology, as always and only embattled, nor to shut down the possibilities of friendly alliances or of some version of "peace." I use *war* to emphasize the seriousness of my engagement with the issues, the depth of my commitment to a methodology that can change the way that scholarship is done in the discipline of rhetoric and composition.

Works Cited

Anzaldúa, Gloria. 1987. *Borderlands/La Frontera: The New Mestiza.* San Francisco: Aunt Lute Books.

Baudrillard, Jean. 1975. *The Mirror of Production.* Trans. Mark Poster. St. Louis: Telos.

Berlin, Jim. 1993. "Composition Studies and Cultural Studies: Collapsing Boundaries." *Into the Field: Sites of Composition Studies.* Ed. Ann Ruggles Gere. New York: MLA, 99–116.

Bernal, Martin. 1987. *Black Athena: The Afroasiatic Roots of Classical Civilization; Volume 1: The Fabrication of Ancient Greece.* New Brunswick: Routledge.

Bruchac, Joseph. 1993. "Notes of a Translator's Son." *Growing Up Native American: An Anthology.* Ed. Patricia Riley. New York: William Morrow & Co., 237–246.

Dorris, Michael. 1987. "Indians on the Shelf." *The American Indian and the Problem of History.* Ed. Calvin Martin. New York: Oxford University Press, 98–105.

Durham, Jimmie. 1992. "Cowboys and . . . : Notes on Art, Literature, and American Indians in the Modern American Mind." *The State of Native America: Genocide, Colonization, and Resistance.* Ed. M. Annette Jaimes. Boston: South End Press, 423–438.

Gould, Janice. 1992. "The Problem of Being 'Indian': One Mixed-Blood's Dilemma." *Decolonizing the Subject: The Politics of Gender in Women's Autobiography.* Eds. Sedonie Smith and Julia Watson. Minneapolis: University of Minnesota Press, 81–87.

Krupat, Arnold (ed.). 1993. *New Voices in Native American Literary Criticism.* Washington, DC: Smithsonian Institution Press.

————. 1992. *Ethnocriticism: Ethnography, History, Literature.* Berkeley: University of California Press.

Lyotard, Jean-François, and Jean Loup Thebaud. 1985. *Just Gaming.* Trans. Wlad Godzich. Minneapolis: University of Minnesota Press.

Moss, Beverly. 1994. "Theory, Theories, Politics, and Journeys." *Writing Theory and Critical Theory.* Eds. John Clifford and John Schilb. New York: MLA, 341–347.

Rose, Wendy. 1993. *Going to War with All My Relations.* Flagstaff, AZ: Entrada Books.

————. 1992. "The Great Pretenders: Further Reflections on Whiteshamanism." *The State of Native America: Genocide, Colonization, and Resistance.* Ed. M. Annette Jaimes. Boston: South End Press, 403–421.

Sequoya, Jana. 1993. "How (!) Is An Indian?: A Contest of Stories." *New Voices in Native American Literary Criticism.* Ed. Arnold Krupat. Washington, DC: Smithsonian Institution Press, 453–473.

Sullivan, Patricia A. 1992. "Feminism and Methodology in Composition Studies." *Methods and Methodology in Composition Research.* Eds. Gesa Kirsch and Patricia A. Sullivan. Carbondale: Southern Illinois University Press, 37–61.

Villanueva, Victor, Jr. 1994. "'Rhetoric Is Politics,' Said the Ancient. 'How Much So,' I Wonder." *Writing Theory and Critical Theory.* Eds. John Clifford and John Schilb. New York; MLA, 327–334.

Vizenor, Gerald. 1994. *Manifest Manners: Postindian Warriors of Survivance.* Hanover, NH: Wesleyan University Press.

———— (ed.). 1989. *Narrative Chance: Postmodern Discourse on Native American Indian Literatures.* Albuquerque: University of New Mexico Press.

————. 1990. *Crossbloods: Bone Courts, Bingo, and Other Reports.* Minneapolis: University of Minnesota Press.

2

News-Surfing the Race Question: Of Bell Curves, Words, and Rhetorical Metaphors

Meta G. Carstarphen

In late 1994, *The Bell Curve: Intelligence and Class Structure in American Life* was published, provoking a media debate like few others about the role of race in our society. Divided into four parts, plus an extensive appendix, *The Bell Curve* sparked the strongest protest because of its third section, entitled "The National Context." Here, the authors discussed ethnic differences, cognitive ability, IQ, and other variables associated with native intelligence. Throwing down the gauntlet at the section's beginning, the authors asserted that "ethnic differences in cognitive ability . . . are real and have consequences" (Herrnstein and Murray, 269). Furthermore, they advanced definitions and premises about race that in and of themselves are arguable:

> There are differences between races, and they are the rule, not the exception. That assertion may seem controversial to some readers, but it verges on tautology: Races are by definition groups of people who differ in characteristic ways. Intellectual fashion has dictated that all differences must be denied except the absolutely undeniable differences in appearance, but nothing in biology says this should be so. (272)

Responses to *The Bell Curve* were swift, energetic and, most importantly, pervasive in the media. In 1994, according to its own electronic database, the *New York Times* published forty-six items about *The Bell Curve* from October to December. The following year, the newspaper published fifty-four additional articles, commentaries, and reviews. Of course, these numbers simply reflect the attention paid by only one media entity, the *Times*. However, newspapers, magazines, and talk shows across the country focused similar spotlights on discussions of race and intelligence.

How does one book spawn such attention and become the catalyst for media frenzy? Reflecting a national schizophrenia about race in our society, this book was more important for the symbolic occasion it represented to discuss race than for its actual ideas. The power of these ideas, however, gained their currency through a media-amplified process of "news-surfing," where concepts are passed along a chain of mediated public discourse. Such a process allows complicated messages and attractive fallacies to permeate societal discourse with speed and intensity, while at the same time often skimming key intellectual surfaces.

Race Words: Now and Then

In his movie based on *The Autobiography of Malcolm X,* director Spike Lee depicts a life-changing moment for the late activist that began with the reading of a common dictionary. Challenged to look up the definitions of *black* and *white* in a standard prison-owned reference book, Malcolm made some uncomfortable discoveries. He noted that the meanings for *black* were uniformly negative, while those for *white* were positive. Although the episode is at least partly apocryphal, no doubt the insight alluded to, along with an acceptance of the philosophically "pro-black" Nation of Islam, led Malcolm X to structure a rhetoric based on a reversal of these connotative polarities. Thus, *black* became symbolic of all that was positive, and *white* became emblematic of all that was negative.

Anyone conducting a similar search through a contemporary dictionary is going to find the same connotative distinctions between *black* and *white* that Malcolm X did fifty years ago. For instance, according to *The American Heritage Dictionary,* some of the most common meanings ascribed to *black* when it is used as an adjective include "having little or no light," "soiled, as from soot; dirty," "evil," "wicked," and "cheerless and depressing; gloomy." By contrast, definitions ascribed to *white* when it is used as an adjective include "pale gray; silvery and lustrous," "bloodless; blanched," and "unsullied" or "pure."

Despite the fact that the meanings of *black* and *white* have become so entrenched in modern discourse as signifiers of extreme opposites, an etymological investigation of these two words, as well as other "race" words, demonstrates just how fluid definitions have been over the centuries. The hunt begins with the clues indicated in the previous entries, which cite the Old English words *blaec* and *hwit* as the origins for the words *black* and *white*. Chronologically, the Old English period is commonly agreed to encompass the years from 449 AD to 1066 AD. The beginning of this period notes the withdrawal of the

Roman Empire from the British Isles and its ensuing occupation by the Germanic ethnic groups of Angles, Saxons, and Jutes; by the end of this period, the Battle of Hastings had been fought, which introduced the Norman, or French, conquerors to early England. The Middle English period begins with the Norman Conquest of 1066—marked by a heavy influence of French and Latinate vocabularies and word forms on the native Germanic dialects—and is generally conceded to have ended with the start of Modern English around 1500.

According to Joseph T. Shipley in the *Dictionary of Word Origins,* both *blaec* and *hwit* existed in the early Anglo-Saxon languages that partly shaped contemporary English, but he notes that the word *blac* was a more common interpretant for *white,* a word that was very similar to *blaec.* As he notes with some irony, "Persons that say things are as different as *black* and *white* might be surprised at how alike these two are. Both were associated in the early mind with absence of color. *Black* is AS [Anglo-Saxon] *blaec;* but AS *blac* is *white"* (1945, 48). Shipley continues to develop the idea of the sameness of black and white by pointing out that evidence remains of this early close association in such words as *bleach, bleak, blanch, blank,* and *blanket*—all of which have incorporated in some way the earliest concept of "whitening," loss of color, or loss of light.

Cross-checking of the words *black* and *white* and their subsequent Old English equivalents, using Gregory K. Jember's *English–Old English, Old English–English Dictionary,* verifies and even amplifies Shipley's observations (1975, 9). *Black* translates into Old English equivalents *blaec, sweart,* and *wann;* words that offer variant interpretations from "black" to "dull black" to "dark." *White* has several equivalents: *blac, beorht, hwit, leohte, leoht* (87). These vary in meaning from *blac's* "bright," "light," and "white" to *hwit's* "light," "luminous," and "white." It is unclear why, over the years, *hwit* became the preferred signifier for white, but the one-time closeness of *blaec* and *blac* show that not only were the words for *black* and *white* nearly identical in form, but they were also quite similar in connotation.

Also, significantly, there is no etymological evidence that either word was used to describe people. Arguably, the early Germanic people may not have had substantial enough contact with visibly "darker" peoples to need such a label, but, equally important, they apparently felt no need to refer to themselves by coloration either. This absence, as well as later etymological evidence where color words do show up as synonyms for people, suggests that these kinds of usages developed concurrently and in opposition to each other.

By contrast, such words were used by the Roman conquerors of early England, as indicated in the *Oxford Latin Dictionary,* and the association is revealing (Glare 1982). The basic word for black is *niger,* which has a masculine form *nigra* and a plural form *nigrum.* Among the meanings associated with *niger* are "dark in colour" and "having a dark skin or complexion, swarthy, dusky, or having black hair." Closely related to *niger* are the words *Nigris* and

Nigritarum. The former word translates as the name for "a great river of western Africa, prob[ably] the Niger," and the latter as a plural name for "a tribe living on the banks of the river Nigris (probably south of the modern Timbuktu)." The hegemony of these three words shows a clear affiliation between *black* and African peoples, and indicates an origin for words that eventually became part of the English lexicon as signifiers for people of African descent. The most obvious descendants of these words are *Negro,* which up until the late 1960s was the preferred appellation for African Americans, and *nigger,* which still persists as a pejorative term for African Americans.

Geography's Primacy

The connections between *Niger* and the continent of Africa are clear, and it is this "fixedness" of color to people and to geography that helps illumine some differences between how ancient peoples defined themselves and others, and how we do. In the example of *Niger,* it is not completely clear whether the concept of color preceded the naming of the region, or whether the region and its people gave new definition to a word already associated with the color black. Nevertheless, the identification of *Niger* with a narrowly defined portion of Africa demonstrates a geographic perspective on peoples and their characteristics that would become a primary tool for observation and reportage used by later European explorers to the African continent. But it is also significant that *Niger* was not the only word used to describe African peoples, and that it appeared not to be a universal label for all indigenous Africans. For example, according to *Cassell's New Latin Dictionary, Afer,* later to become *Africae,* was used to mean ". . . Africa, especially in the narrow sense of the district around Carthage" (Simpson 1960). Why Carthage? This centering on a region on the northern tip of the African continent and an area bounded, as was ancient Rome, by the Mediterranean Sea reflects something of the long and often stormy history between the two cultures.

In addition to Afer and Niger, Romans apparently recognized yet another distinct region on the African continent: Aegyptus, or what we now refer to as Egypt. These designations may not exhaust all the regional names the Romans assigned to various parts of the African continent, but they do point out that there was not merely one single appellation for Africans, and suggest strongly some recognition of the diversity of cultures inhabiting these areas. Moreover, this "naming" of these three regions seems wholly consistent with geographic identifications of other cultures north of Rome; examples include "Europa" for the continent of Europe and "Britannia" for Great Britain.

Britannia was not considered a monolithic region either; it included Britain, including Albion (England) and Caledonia (Scotland). It is also interesting to note that *Albion,* like *Niger,* seems to have its meaning connected to region *and* color, because it is closely related to the word *albus,* meaning "white; light-colored, light-skinned, fair" (Glare 1982, 93). For the Romans, such an appellation for the pale-skinned, blond-haired British forebears might have seemed wholly appropriate.

Many scholars, like Gertrude Jobes (1961), identify *Albion* with the "white caps of the sea" or the "white cliffs of Dover." Indeed, many contemporary visitors to the British Isles can attest to the chalk-like appearance of the famous Dover cliffs. But Jobes also cites *Albion* as a name in Greek myth for a giant son of Poseidon, god of the sea, who discovered the British Isles and was slain by Hercules. This additional coincidence would seem to give another "sea-based" rationale for the Albion/England connection.

Were the Poseidon/Albion connection more certain, the association of *Albion* with the "white caps" of the sea or "white cliffs" overlooking the sea might be more credible as the only justification for the Roman association of England with "whiteness." However, the legendary comment of Pope Gregory the Great, as recorded by the Venerable Bede, may confirm that the Romans were struck by the countenances of the Anglo-Saxons as well. Reportedly, the Cleric became inspired to send a mission to Christianize England in 597 AD after noticing captive Angles being sold in a Roman marketplace as slaves, where he commented: "Alas! What pity that the author of darkness is possessed of men of such *fair* countenances . . ." (Zesmer 1961, 9) [emphasis mine].

Examining this fragmentary evidence of color words and their associations with people in Roman and early English languages helps shed light on some of the realities of "racial" concepts. People of European and English descent have not always been considered "white" people, and all Africans have not always been considered "black" people. With the exception of *Niger* and possibly *Albion,* color seems not to have been a factor at all in the naming and identification of people, and certainly did not have the universal resonances that *white* and *black* carry today. But this began to change dramatically just as the European Renaissance was becoming the defining experience for much of the known world and just as Middle English was evolving into a more codified "modern" language. The *Oxford Dictionary of English Etymology* notes the appearance in the sixteenth century of a new word, *blackamoor,* which was understood as a universally applicable label for any "negro," which itself was a word borrowed from the Spanish, meaning "black," and originating from the Latin *niger* (Onions 1966).

A Shift from Place to Metaphor

Ernest Klein (1966), in *A Comprehensive Etymological Dictionary of the English Language,* further explains *blackamoor* as a compound "of black and Moor." A Moor was defined as "a native of Morocco," as well as "one of the Moslem invaders of Spain or their descendants." Here, region and religion merge to inform the meaning of *Moor,* giving it some specificity, but *blackamoor* was not restricted to any regional boundary except the broadest of ones: the continent of Africa. Klein's dictionary, which defines *blackamoor* as "a

Negro," leaves unexplained the specific construction of *blackamoor* other than to note that it is a compound of "*black* and *moor.*" It also defines *Negro* as "a member of the black race of Africa" (1037).

However, it seems evident that this word reveals the beginning of a figurative conception of "race" that would model subsequent naming of ethnicities, especially people of color. Essentially, this model establishes the criterion of color—not culture or geography—as the preeminent characteristic of identification. Moreover, the use of color is relative and comparative. *Blackamoor* seems understandable, thus, not as a compound of *black* and *moor,* but rather as a contraction of the implied argument that this person being referred to was "as black as a Moor." And, to have said that someone was "a[s] black [as] a Moor" was to create a simple paradigm for communicating an identity not only about that individual, but also about an entire group whose specific regional origin would be unknown or seen as unimportant. Thus, the connotative loop encircling color and ethnicity became closed and self-perpetuating in the word *blackamoor* in a way that had not been evident as little as a hundred years before the start of the sixteenth century. "Race" and "color" words first appear to become part of the English lexicon between 1400 and 1500, just as the European exploitation of African people was taking form.

From Color to Race

However carefully the use of "color" words, or the lack of it, can be traced throughout language histories of Latin and early English forms, such a trail does not entirely explain how differences were measured among people of different ethnic and cultural traditions. Certainly, today's prevailing logic about "color" having been a universal and immediate way of distinguishing people throughout time seems weak, for it is obvious that for the most part the highly eclectic Roman Empire distinguished people by region and by culture. Apparently, so did the forebears of modern Britain populations, if the Old English text of *Beowulf* is any indication. The unknown author/transcriber recounts an epic tale of war, strife, and competition among early Germanic tribes by referring to the varying groups according to their cultural origins as Danes, Geats, Frisians, and the like. An attitude of cultural chauvinism, rather than "racial" prejudice, seems operative. Furthermore, tracing backwards through etymological evidence from today's commonly accepted definition of *race* does not lead back to objective correlatives in ancient languages: *race* in today's English simply does not translate into a synonymous word.

Shipley's (1945) *Dictionary of Word Origins* once again illustrates that the path from ancient languages to modern usage is often a crooked one, as his investigation points to three separate linguistic influences on the modern notion of "race" that, at first glance, seem to have little in common with each other or with their contemporary cousin: the "trial of speed" from the early Germanic languages or Teutonic dialects; the idea of "a line" from the Italian and the Old High German; and the notion of a "root," which most nearly comes to English through Old French and Latin. Adding to the mystery is the fact that, again, according to dictionaries for Old English and Latin languages, there were no words indigenous to these tongues that seemed to encompass the overarching meaning that has been attributed to *race* today—this despite some very specific words expressing some sense of communal differences.

For instance, there were two words in Old English that approximated the idea of what it meant to belong to a nation or a special group: *byrdu* and *cynn*. Jember (1975) defines *byrdu* as "race, nature by birth" and *cynn* as "family, race." However, because earlier dictionary entries have shown no clear etymology between *race* as we define it today and a parent word in Germanic languages, it seems apparent that the addition of *race* as part of the definitions for both *byrdu* and *cynn* are most accurately a contemporary scholar's attempt to bridge the obvious gap between how historical peoples measured "racial" difference and how we do.

Moreover, *byrdu* as "nature by birth" and *cynn* as "family" seem most complementary to the kinds of alliances portrayed in the literature from the Old English period. Without a sense of "race" as we now know it, Teutonic peoples nevertheless had strong sensibilities for family, clan, and kinship ties, which these words express. Apparently, the ever combative Angles, Saxons, Jutes, Geats, and other Germanic tribes clearly did not see themselves as all part of one "racial" heritage, although there were some similarities among them in language, ritual, and custom. Ironically, it took the Norman Conquest of 1066 AD to provide the impetus, sustained over a long enough period, that would impel the warring Germanic tribes into a sense of Anglo-Saxon unity, a sense of "English" national identity.

Similarly, citizens of the expansive Roman Empire, which at various times encompassed territories around the Mediterranean, the continent of Africa, and the British Isles, described what we might call today racial differences in a way that emphasized national origin and culture. Although one of the key words of origin for the contemporary word *race* is the Latin word *radix,* another word more nearly describes difference and separation: *genus.* Even today, *genus* thrives in scientific nomenclature as a label of identification and separation of one form of life from another; to know the genus of a living organism is to say that it is classified with others most like it.

Even allowing for an intrusion of the contemporary idea of "race" into these explanations, the concept of "genus" incorporates many of the same divisive ideas we think of today when we consider *race. Genus* also seems to develop on the notions of familial and geographical similarities as being the basis for these classifications, much as *byrdu* and *cynn* do.

But *radix,* not *genus,* is the Latin word of origin for today's *race* word, accounting for its truest linguistic heritage. Of the five interpretations cited for *radix* in the *Oxford Latin Dictionary,* hardly any of them seem applicable to ethnicity:

1. root of plant or tree
2. root (regarded as giving stability and solidarity)
3. basal portion of the parts of the body (hair, teeth)
4. lower or extreme part of anything
5. source, origin, root of anything; source of a family breed; stock (1571).

The last notation, suggesting a usage for *race* as the "source of a family breed," is the only place where concepts of family or kinship seem to resemble anything like contemporary notions of ethnic grouping. On the face of it, *radix* seems a much less adequate label for "racial" difference than does *genus,* which has an objectified approach to the clear-cut classification of living things.

But what if, save for skin color and hair texture, there were no objective, clear-cut divisions of human beings, no objective lines of demarcation that could clarify "subordinate kinds or varieties?" Then would subjective ones do?

Circuitous though the path has been, *race* could only have triumphed as the preferred signifier of human difference if the various links informing its origin were put together very subjectively and very creatively. As indicated by previous citations, the three strands of meaning that seemed to converge within *race* were a "trial of speed," a "line," and a "root" (Shipley 1945, 294). The first of these three most comfortably informs the meaning of *race* when it is used contemporarily to denote a competition of some kind, as in a foot, horse, or car race. But a rapid sprint across virtually any surface except concrete should leave a clear, visible line. Thus, the connection between the first and the second meanings is not so hard to contemplate. More challenging is the notion of *race* as "root," yet this is probably the connotation that is the most illuminating as a conceptual forebear of the modern idea of "race." Derivative of the Old French word *rais,* meaning root, the English version of *race* as root was probably in use for much of the Norman-dominated period of Middle English. According to *The Oxford Dictionary of English Etymology, race* first appeared in usage as a signifier for ethnicity in the sixteenth century—the same period that *black-amoor* appeared in written usage as well (Onions 1966). But *race* was also concurrently in use to mean "root," as in "root of ginger" (735), a more customary and frequent definition at that time.

Renaissance dramas, pulsating with the idioms of their audiences and reflecting popular ideas of the day, are revealing measures of this duality in the meanings of *race.* For example, in *The Winter's Tale* by William Shakespeare, a character, The Clown, contemplates what spices to purchase for his master's upcoming sheep-shearing feast, and uses *race* in a customary way, as a root, when he refers to "a *race* or two of ginger" [emphasis mine].

Although specific dating of Shakespearean dramas is often conjectural, *The Winter's Tale* is believed to have been performed around 1610–1611. Another

Shakespearean drama given a similar dating is *The Tempest.* In it, the character Miranda castigates Caliban, described as a "savage and deformed slave," and in her rebuff uses *race* in a way that is synonymous with "nature," as she up-braids Caliban for his "[re]vil'd *race*" [emphasis mine].

Here, Caliban's "vile nature" is the basis of his failure to be transformed by Miranda's humanizing efforts; something essential within his very being has defined him more assiduously than any environmental influence could. The man/beast Caliban has become "rooted" in the circumstances of his origins and his birth. Significantly, Caliban is an *indigenous* being of the unnamed island upon which the events of *The Tempest* transpire; all others, including Miranda, are stranded there as a result of uncontrollable events. When examined side by side, the twin connotations of *race* during the English Renaissance reveal a symbiotic formula that was pivotal in the evolution of the modern word *race*. Accordingly, these ideas set the foundation for the emergence of modern "ra-cial" ideas of separation and difference.

Thus, the essence of *race* was initially not in the concept of separateness (although that certainly was an outgrowth), but rather lay in the notion that there existed certain pure and unchanging characteristics, endowed by Nature, that could be recognized as being so fundamental to a man's character that they were part of his past, present, and future. As such, "race" was seen as a matter of lineage, as something that had been given in birth and was capable of being passed on through future births. It was also a matter of *place,* as well as *blood,* and the long tradition previously seen in Greek, Roman, and Early English lit-eratures of identifying people with the land from which they come was still a popular notion. Caliban's "race" was as much a function of the "soil" on which he was born, just as, by implication, Miranda's "good nature" was possible be-cause she was *not* a native of his island.

The metaphorical power of such an image linking man and plant must have seemed eminently seductive to the Renaissance mind. On the threshold of a renewed interest in man's place in the natural world, the idea of man's "race" nourishing him just as a plant's roots were sustaining it must have seemed quite logical. Even in modern times, the association is not farfetched. Probably more than any other contemporary author, the late Alex Haley immortalized the con-cept of familial "roots" through the writing of his own family history. What a supreme irony it is that Haley made the word *root* symbolic of the recapturing of African history when it was used some four centuries ago to sever and de-mean that very history.

Ultimately, there was a final, compelling factor that helped engender the conditions in which a rhetoric of racism would be created. For without the cat-aclysmic, history-changing consequences of the African slave trade, the need to define *race* would never have existed. Moreover, the massive transport of what would eventually become millions of human beings from Africa, and their subsequent dispersion to many geographic locations, conceptually invalidated the authority that "place" had previously given to identity. The metaphor of race was needed by European and British enslavers to justify a practice that from its beginning had its detractors, long before the pseudo-science of racial genetics (as reinvigorated by *The Bell Curve*) could be created by social scientists and intellectuals. "Race" as a figurative concept had to form the basis of a powerful rhetoric of racism that could sustain the argument of "racial" difference in terms that would make its basic premises inviolate and supremely natural.

To Contemporary News

Carl Rowan, a nationally syndicated columnist and African American journalist, was one of the many commentators who reacted strongly to the rise of neo-Nazi activities in Germany. Noting similarities between the expressions of "race" hatred in the United States and in contemporary Germany, Rowan made these observations and assertions:

> We Americans should deplore, but without sanctimony, this resurgence of hate violence in Germany. We must view it with two truisms in mind:
>
> 1) Bigotry, ethnic and *racial hatreds, the dark side of man's nature, can never be expunged from human life. It can only be controlled.* (emphasis mine)
>
> 2) In every nation, town or place, wise and brave political leadership is the key to restraining the mob mentality and retaining relative tranquility. (1992, 31A)

In this statement, Rowan articulated two dueling axioms that both impel and cripple media writing about race. On the one hand, Rowan posits the hope that enlightened leadership can make a difference in human relationships. On the other hand, he suggests that even the best of "wise and brave political leadership" will not be sufficient to override the inherent intransigence of human will concerning race. The danger of this strategy is that it becomes a self-fulfilling prophecy and philosophy. Tying man's inability to avoid "racism" to irrevocable patterns of natural design causes assertions, especially negative ones, about "race" relations to resound with the similitude of truth.

In the case of Rowan's italicized statement, the view that "racial" hatred is an indelible mark on the soul and history of mankind is one that is universally propagated in popular news discourse—and the cynicism it expresses is compatible with the aura of skepticism that journalists assiduously cultivate. An "objective" realist, such as a trained journalist, must be able to interpret "racial" matters without the encumbrance of unsubstantiated idealism or too obvious a natural bias. But the premise on which Rowan's argument and countless others rest—the idea that there has been a millennium of human history marked by "racial" prejudice and that such hatreds are instinctual—comprises the essential fallacy undergirding contemporary rhetoric about "race." Until that fallacy is addressed, all "racial" discourse is meaningless.

The Racial Enthymeme and Embedded Fallacy

In the Rowan statement, the application of the rhetorical fallacy of "race" occurs in the basic unit of construction informing all argument—the rhetorical syllogism:

> Bigotry, ethnic and *racial hatreds, the dark side of man's nature, can never be expunged from human life. It can only be controlled.*

Such a "hasty generalization" is an example of the type of broad and sweeping statement that often characterizes journalistic discourse about "race," yet which just as often takes on the weight of "fact" because of the authority of both writer and medium behind it. To analyze the fallacy behind such a statement, it is useful to format it according to the structure of the rhetorical syllogism.

James McBurney's 1939 analysis of the rhetorical syllogism, or enthymeme, is a definitive study of how Aristotle, who rhetoricians credit with developing the concept of the enthymeme, saw its role in formal argument structure. Subsequently, in a 1959 article, Lloyd Bitzer updated McBurney's observations in some key ways. While agreeing that the enthymeme was usually missing one component of the typical three-part syllogism, Bitzer argued that this missing term was not the distinguishing feature between enthymemes and scientific, or logical, syllogisms. Rather, this omission was a deliberate construct resulting from the rhetor's knowledge that the missing term, or assumption, was intuitively shared by his or her audience.

In a classic example of a formal, or logical, syllogism, the following components of the syllogism show how a rhetorical enthymeme proceeds from a generalized statement, to a specific application derivative of the first statement, to a "new" assertion that has built its legitimacy from the veracity of the first two terms. This process of deduction, which moves from a broad idea to a specific conclusion, is "formally" valid as long as there are three terms that follow this structure:

Major Premise: All human beings(A) are mortal(B).

Minor Premise: Socrates(C) is a human being(A).

Conclusion: Socrates(C) is mortal(B).

If written as a formula, the syllogism would read "ABC, ACB." The major premise is restated and the "B" and "C" terms, equally valid, are interchangeable.

However, logic—or the appearance of it—can be deceptively convincing if erroneous assumptions comprise the essential terms of the enthymeme. Thus, although an argument can have formal validity, it can lack truthful validity if its minor premise is false. A witty example of such a fallacy was cleverly written by Eugene Ionesco in his play, *Rhinoceros,* which mocks the tendency of falsehood to masquerade as truth under the disguise of a logical presentation (1981, 488). The text is reconstructed in the form of a syllogism:

Major Premise:	All cats(A) die(B).
Minor Premise:	Socrates(C) is dead(B).
Conclusion:	Socrates(C) is a cat(A).

Here, the formula is "ABC, BCA," not the logically valid "ABC, ACB." The "B" and "A" terms of the syllogism have switched places. However, by generating an irrelevant fact ("Socrates is dead") as a "B" term, and making it parallel in meaning to a relevant "C" term fact ("All cats die"), the final statement "A" of the syllogism has the appearance of truth: "Socrates is a cat."

When the same rhetorical test is applied to the Rowan statement, the pattern of the fallacy becomes more evident:

Major Premise:	Bigotry and ethnic and racial hatreds(A) are the dark side of human nature(B).
Minor Premise:	Every man(C) has a dark side to his nature because he is human(B).
Conclusion:	Every man(C) has bigotry and ethnic and racial hatred in him(A).

Separately, the ideas that "man has a dark side" and "racial prejudice is part of man's dark side" may have some truth, but more clarifying details are needed before such an assertion should pass the test of truth. What, for instance, is meant by "man's dark side?" What, specifically, are "bigotry, race hatred, and prejudice?" Are they attitudes, behaviors, or emotions? Is there a fundamental consensus on the definition of these key terms—some shared truths—that would allow such an argument to proceed? All too often, despite these inconsistencies, the racial enthymeme succeeds *precisely* because the same fallacious ideas about "race" are shared.

Just as in Ionesco's logical whimsy, the racial enthymeme impedes clarity on "race" by first making sweeping generalizations about human nature. Then, it gives its conclusion the appearance of logic and truth by aligning two plausible but fundamentally unproven or incomplete assertions in a parallel relationship.

The notion that racism is inevitable and that race classification—as we define it—holds unquestionable sway over our actions, thoughts, and beliefs is the fallacious "cat" of our modern discourse. The ethnic differences among human beings count for something, to be sure, but exactly what race is and what it means to our current discourse is subject to frenzied debate. And in the madcap pace of modern communication, no one bothers to take the time to challenge key premises or define important terms, least of all in discourse about the widely discussed but easily generalized subject of "race."

Can We Talk?

Every day, society seems to be bombarded by media messages about "race," and few of them seem positive. There is a general malaise about the ability of people to cope with ethnic differences, and many people, from young to old, feel hopeless about the possibility of transcending a legacy of bitterness, violence, and hatred.

Currently, virtually all discourse about "race"—including all forms of verbal, written, and electronic media communication—has repeated the same false message that was created more than five hundred years ago. Although rhetoric about "race" is certainly not new to the twentieth century, factors that are peculiar to this century are the forms of mass media that have proliferated since 1900 and their influences on our discourse and our society. As the architects of a "literature of fact," media discourse-makers have helped obscure the true story of "race" in two ways: by using the figurative to represent objective conditions, and by forcing news about ethnicity into the five-hundred-year-old metaphor about "race."

Discourse scholars and practitioners should unite for some creative brainstorming on the lexicon and create alternative ways of talking about ethnic differences. Moreover, broader definitions of *race* and *racism* should be promoted that highlight their subjective qualities instead of their objective consequences. Journalists, especially, have an obligation to clarify these terms when they write them and to insist on clarity when their "sources" use these terms liberally.

As discouraging as these times are, the good news is that modern societies are in the midst of an important paradigm shift about ethnicity. Rhetoric is at the heart of this shift, for the impending changes are not simply about changing people's feelings for each other, but also demanding that the language used reflects the realities of modern living.

Works Cited

Bitzer, Lloyd F. 1959. "Aristotle's Enthymeme Revisited." *Quarterly Journal of Speech.* 45: 399–408.

Cooper, Lane (trans.). 1932. *The Rhetoric of Aristotle.* Englewood Cliffs: Prentice-Hall.

Glare, P. G. W. (ed.). 1982. *Oxford Latin Dictionary.* New York: Oxford University Press.

Herrnstein, Richard, and Charles Murray. 1994. *The Bell Curve: Intelligence and Class Structure in American Life.* New York: Basic Books.

Ionesco, Eugene. 1981. *Rhinoceros.* Derek Prouse (trans.). *Nine Plays of the Modern Theater.* Howard Clurman (ed.). New York: Grove Press. 471–572.

Jember, Gregory K. (ed.), with John C. Carrell, Robert P. Lundquist, Barbara M. Olds, and Raymond P. Tripp, Jr. 1975. *English–Old English, Old English–English Dictionary.* Boulder: Westview Press.

Jobes, Gertrude. 1961. *Dictionary of Mythology, Folklore and Symbols.* 3 Vols. New York: Scarecrow Press.

Klein, Ernest. 1966. *A Comprehensive Etymological Dictionary of the English Language (Dealing with the Origin of Words and Their Sense Development Thus Illustrating the History of Civilization and Culture).* 2 Vols. Amsterdam: Elsevier Publishing Co.

McBurney, James H. 1939. "The Place of the Enthymeme in Rhetorical Theory." *Speech Monographs.* 3: 49–74.

McQuade, Donald (gen. ed.). 1987. *The Harper American Literature, Vol. 1*. New York: Harper & Row.

Onions, C. T. (ed.), with G. W. S. Friedrichsen and R. W. Burchfield. 1966. *The Oxford Dictionary of English Etymology*. Oxford: Clarendon Press.

Rowan, Carl. 1992. "Germany, the U.S., and Hatred." *Dallas Morning News*. December 3, 1992. 31A.

Shipley, Joseph T. 1945. *Dictionary of Word Origins*. New York: Philosophical Library.

Simpson, D. P. (ed.) 1960. *Cassell's New Latin Dictionary, Latin–English, English–Latin*. New York: Funk & Wagnalls.

The American Heritage Dictionary. 1982. 2nd College Edition. Boston: Houghton Mifflin.

Zesmer, David M. 1961. *Guide to English Literature: From Beowulf Through Chaucer and Medieval Drama*. With bibliographies by Stanley B. Greenfield. New York: Barnes & Noble.

3

Terrorists, Madmen, and Religious Fanatics?: Revisiting Orientalism and Racist Rhetoric

Anissa Janine Wardi

"Tell me what you'd like to do with these towelheads," implored radio personality Howie Carr in the wake of the April 19, 1995, bombing of the Alfred P. Murrah Federal Building in Oklahoma City (Grunwald 1995, 1). Responding to media reports that Middle Eastern–looking men were thought to be responsible for the tragedy, Carr articulated a position that incited violence against Arabs, Arab Americans, and Muslims. As people around the country struggled to make sense of this tragedy, Arab Americans and Muslims mourned with them, while at the same time fearing for their own safety. Knowing the anti-Arab sentiment that exists in America, and fearing the backlash that the implication of Arab involvement would incite, Arab Americans and Muslims maintained a low profile during the days following the bombing. Many in the Arab American community feared that, if indeed, Arabs were responsible, there would be an onslaught of hate crimes directed at innocent Muslims and Arab Americans throughout the nation.

Although the immediate concern that Arabs were responsible for this crime was allayed, the question of how we as a society attempted to apprehend this tragedy and the subsequent ramifications of this narrative deserve closer scrutiny. The racist discourse that ensued in the aftermath of the Oklahoma bombing went largely unnoticed and therefore uncontested. To read the reaction to this cultural sign, it is necessary to contextualize this narrative within the larger historical/cultural landscape. The rhetorical strategies deployed during that crisis exemplify Orientalist discourse as defined by Edward Said (1978)

31

in his seminal text, *Orientalism.* Said holds that one of the "principal dogmas of Orientalism . . . is the absolute and systematic difference between the West, which is rational, developed, humane, superior, and the Orient, which is aberrant, undeveloped, inferior" (300). Orientalism is an ideological assumption held by the West that actually enables the domination and control of the Orient, thus impacting the lives of Arab people.

Realizing the crucial role that language assumes in the creation and maintenance of Western hegemony, Said argues that "without examining Orientalism as a discourse, one cannot possibly understand the enormously systematic discipline by which European culture was able to manage—and even produce—the Orient . . ." (3). Literal and metaphoric naming underscores the import of Said's claim that language is the vehicle through which domination is fully realized. Arabs, as merely one representative group, have been defined by the Western colonial gaze. The very term that many of us use to define ourselves, *Middle Eastern,* clearly smacks of Western colonization for, as Joanna Kadi (1994) asserts, "[i]t's a term that could only make sense to white colonizers so certain their existence and homelands were the center of everything that they actually named huge regions of the world in relation to themselves" (xix). This literal naming symbolizes the West's metaphorical defining of Arabs and, by extension, Arab Americans.

One noticeable historical trend in the characterization of Arabs is a move from exoticizing the Middle East as a land of mystery, danger, and illicit sexuality—which are all represented, for instance, in the familiar narrative of the Arab man's insatiable lust for "white" women—to the demonization of Arabs and Islam. This is not to suggest that the former narrative is out of circulation; rather, it actually created a narrative space for the current utter dehumanization of Arabs, and is very much still in existence. Arab identities have been inscribed by the West to the point where the terms *Arab* and *Middle Easterner* no longer simply denote ethnic identification markers; rather, they have become what Roland Barthes (1957) labeled "mythic signifiers" (121) that transcend the realities of continental affiliation. The one-dimensional renderings of Arab men and women are manifest in our societal discourse and used as cultural currency by virtue of the fact that these images are widely held in the West as valid representations of Arab people.

The proliferation of denigrating Arab stereotypes in the West is so ingrained that the body of an Arab man is reduced to the symbolic embodiment of evil: the bloodthirsty madman/terrorist. One example of this widespread racism is seen in an Arab sheik mask that a prominent costume retailer sold. While it is problematic that children are encouraged to "dress up" as Arabs, the fact that the mask was a hideous caricature and was sold under the "Monster Mask" line underscores the severity of this racial dehumanization. Demonizing Arabs as monsters conveys the message that they should be feared as dangerous and violent creatures. Moreover, the fact that the Arab monster mask was the only mask sold by the retailer that demeans an entire group of people speaks to the position of Arabs in America. While Arab men, as this mask represents, are primarily identified as terrorists, they also are constructed as polygamists, patriarchal oppressors, and cruel fathers. Further, these constructions necessarily presume that Arab women are identified as passive, subservient, and dominated. This myth of the universally "subjugated" covered woman is juxtaposed to the Orientalist myth of the erotic harem girl, who is sexually available to men. This second myth, though, also relies on the narrative of patriarchal oppressor. As Michelle Sharif (1994) explains, "[t]he West came to define the harem as a prison for women and their captors as violent Muslim men" (154).

The caricature of Arabs as bloodthirsty villains is so pervasive in America that it has become the master narrative defining the Arab/Arab American people in the West. The vilification of Arabs, which effectively reduces their identities to a trope of evil, is evidenced in the term *terrorist,* which is often used as a metonym for *Arab* in mainstream societal discourse. The representation of Arab peoples and Muslims in American popular culture sheds light on the extent of derogatory stereotyping and provides an important context in which to place the racist rhetoric that accompanied the Oklahoma tragedy.

Movie producers have parlayed the popularity of the Arab villain into major motion pictures. Like *Sesame Street,* in which a picture of an Arab was used to signify the word *danger,* so too do diverse movie genres such as animated features, dramas, and action adventures reflect and reinforce the stereotype of inherent Arab evilness (Michalak 1988, 7). *Not Without My Daughter* is an example of an anti-Islamic narrative which, like anti-Arab films, has gained increasing popularity in the American film industry. Although *Not Without My Daughter* demonizes Muslims and Iranians (who are not Arabs), most Westerners see Middle Easterners as a homogeneous people. The most damaging theme of the film, that American racism toward Iranians and Islam is justified, is established early on.

The beginning of the film presents an idyllic American family: Sally Field portrays a Euro-American woman married to an Iranian-born medical doctor. The husband faces racism from the American doctors at work, as they call the Middle East a barbaric civilization. At this point in the film, the viewer is encouraged to be outraged at these seemingly ignorant aspersions. However, when the family makes a trip to Iran, the racist doctors' sentiments are proven correct. In Iran, the viewer is bombarded by masses of people who are speaking simultaneously. If these people are in fact speaking Farsi, why are they devoiced in this narrative? There are no subtitles provided when groups of people are speaking because their voices, we are to understand, are unimportant. It does not matter what these people are saying because the West knows their collective identity and, thus, their individual existence is nullified.

Iran is portrayed as a backwards, inhumane, violent country that breeds abusive men and passive women. In this "horrible" country, as Sally Field's character refers to it, the husband who was so warm and loving in America becomes an abusive husband and father. At one point in the movie, he slaps his wife, stating, "You're in *my* country now. You're my wife, you do as I say!," thus revealing that his kindness and decency in America were nothing more than a facade masking his "real" Iranian nature, which was waiting to be unleashed. Islam is clearly implicated in the husband's evil transformation: the cross the wife wears around her neck stands in opposition to this so-called heathen religion, thus creating a facile dichotomy of good versus evil.

The West's notion of the mythic Muslim man as abusive patriarch is upheld, while feelings of American patriotism are fostered. The Orientalist idea of the West as civilized and the East as barbaric is evident as the wife accounts for her husband's cruelty by implicating his ethnicity and religion. She states, "I thought of him as an *American;* oh God, he's changed" (emphasis mine). This statement implies that American men are morally superior to Middle Eastern men: the spousal abuse that many Americans believe is so prevalent in the Middle East is portrayed as virtually nonexistent in the West. Indeed, with this statement, the wife articulates still another racist text of the film—namely, that only "white" Christian people are truly American. Those of us who are "others," the film implies, are not really Americans and should not be trusted as such.

Another movie, *Aladdin,* one of Disney's top-grossing films, was reviewed by many critics as a positive step toward so-called multicultural cinema. In reality, the movie appropriated this space of otherness ("Agrabah," the mythical Arab country portrayed in the film) and, in fact, reinscribed Western ethnocentric attitudes. The narrative of Arab violence is established in the film's opening song, which is overtly Orientalist: "Oh, I come from a land from a faraway place where the caravan camels roam. Where they cut off your ear if they don't like your face. It's barbaric, but hey, it's home." [1] These racist lyrics set the tone for the more subtle Orientalist aspects of the film. Aladdin, for example, is chased by street merchants who want to cut off his hands for stealing bread, a common narrative held by Americans who view Islam as teaching this kind of cruelty. Indeed, Aladdin and Princess Jasmine are portrayed as anomalies in this backward, violent country. Unlike the rest of the characters, they speak with American accents and have light skin. They are in fact the literal embodiment of the West and, thus, easily lend themselves to being the heroes of the drama for an American audience. The racial sensibilities of many Westerners are not disrupted as Princess Jasmine is virtually imprisoned in her father's castle with only her pet tiger, Raja, to keep her company. The symbol of the tiger serves a twofold purpose: (1) it adds to the exotic ambiance of the Middle East, and (2) it is used as a measure of Arab humanity, implying as it does that animals are more trustworthy and compassionate than the Arab people.

The frequency with which these images are produced in the mass media and the lack of critical commentary regarding the representations of Arabs and Islam create an accepted portrait of otherness. In turn, this portrait plays a central role in defining and maintaining American politics. The relationship of political rhetoric to the discourse of the mass media is evidenced by Jane Fonda who, in promoting her 1981 film *Rollover,* concretized her film's anti-Arab message: "If we aren't afraid of Arabs, we'd better examine our heads. They have strategic power over us. They are unstable, they are fundamentalists, tyrants, anti-woman, anti-free press. That we have to depend on them is monstrous" (Michalak 1988, 26).

The pervasiveness of this kind of racist discourse not only maintains the West/East hierarchy, but also has moved to the level of racist mythology. The obvious fact that Arab men are not categorically evil has little to do with the powerful cultural ideology this myth has engendered, as is evidenced by the reception of Arab people in America. Regardless of its validity, myth is the foundation of social reality; it is the currency through which we attempt to apprehend complexity. The key property of myth is that this process remains hidden —myths become normative as "objective" ideology and reified through daily exchange. Significantly, this is often a hegemonic exercise whereby the world is ordered according to a racist hierarchy. Further, as Lubiano (1992) states:

> Salient narratives are the means by which sense is made in and of the world; they also provide the means by which those who hold power (or influence the maintenance of power) make or attempt to make sense of the world *for others*. Such narratives are so naturalized, so pushed by the momentum of their ubiquity, that they seem to be reality. That dynamic is the work of ideology. (328–329)

That these myths' constructedness is invisible explains how Arabs and Arab Americans can be reduced to symbolic tropes. Barthes continues by defining an integral property of myth as its ability to "[transform] history into nature" (129). This aspect of myth resonates with the unabashed racist discourse aimed at Arabs and Arab Americans, enabling Westerners, as it does, to confront the Arab "other," purporting to know the identity—the nature—of all Arabs. The media's reporting of the Oklahoma bombing reveals the assumption that Arabs, as a collective people, are known to the West.

Racial stereotyping prevailed as the media described the suspects in the bombing as "Middle Eastern–looking men." Having heard this initial report, I wondered how the store owner who later claimed to have sold fertilizer to Arabs recognized them as such? In other words, what did he think Middle Eastern men look like? The term *Sand Nigger* is used by many people to characterize the Middle Eastern "other," but the ambiguity of this racist epithet conveys little more than a sweeping incrimination of anyone who is not presumed to be "white." This racism not only results in anti-Arab aggression, but also, like the backlash of the Gulf War, victimizes other people of color. For example, during the Gulf War, a pipe bomb exploded at the home of an Indian family presumed to be Iraqi (Eiken and Gorchev 1992, 16). Several men verbally abused a Polynesian Jewish man, calling him (among other things) a "Filthy Arab! Arab pig!" (11). In New York City, a Pakistani man was physically beaten by several men who repeatedly referred to him as an "Arab terrorist" (17). The extent of this racial hegemony is evident in the words of one man who made a death threat to an Arab American community center in Cleveland, Ohio, identifying himself as a representative of the "Aryan people" (11).

Anti-Arab racism, like all forms of racism, is never aimed solely at one group, but rather is fueled by a hatred for all those who are seen as different. There are numerous racist narratives operating in our social discourse regarding the nature of the "other." While a number of these narratives have been challenged, revised, and altered over the years, at this particular historical moment the salient narrative of violence and terrorism attached to the Arab people is highly visible and largely uncontested.

The immediate presumption that three "Middle Eastern–looking" men were responsible for the Oklahoma bombing was widely disseminated by the media and largely accepted by the public, for it resonates with the master narrative of the Arab in Western society. The convergence of the word (the narrative of Arab terrorists) and the picture (the scene of mass destruction in Oklahoma) became the interpretive framework for understanding the tragedy and, therefore, other leads were virtually dismissed by the media. President Clinton's initial reaction to the Oklahoma bombing recalls the assumption that only the "other" could have committed a crime as heinous as this: "Make no mistake, this was an attack on the United States, our way of life, everything we believe in" (Benedetto 1995, 3A). While not literally naming the bombing as an act of foreign aggression, the fact that Clinton read the situation as an attack on "our" way of life silently implies that those who are responsible are not any of "us," but are instead "they," who are not Americans.

This Orientalist discourse was echoed by the countless "Middle East experts" who took this opportunity to warn the public of the Arab mentality—reducing Arabs' humanity by suggesting they are a monolithic people. Prior to learning that the suspects were Euro-American, these experts made a number of claims, all of which suggested that violence is the special domain of Middle Eastern people: "The signature looks Middle Eastern" (Quinn-Judge and Sennott 1995, 24); "You have to say this is certainly their [Islamic fundamentalists] M.O." (Zaldivar and Goldstein 1995, A23); "The Federal Building had the Middle East written all over it" (Shammas 1995, 25); and "This was done with the intent to inflict as many casualties as possible. That is a Middle Eastern trait" (*ADC Times* 1995, 4).

The few newspaper articles that purported to quell the anti-Arab fervor inevitably reinscribed the same narrative. One article entitled, "Experts Say It's Too Early to Assign Blame for Blast on Any One Group," spent the majority of the article citing reasons *for* the incrimination of Arabs and/or Arab Americans (Zaldivar and Goldstein 1995, A23). Despite what the reporters read as a great deal of incriminating evidence, they cautioned the reader not to rush to judgment. However, their own bias belied this warning. Referring to Attorney General Reno's refusal to lay blame on any one group, the article read, "at a White House news conference, Attorney General Reno refused to label the tragedy a terrorist act and would not comment on any aspect of the investigation"

(A23). Because Reno was not implicating Arabs in this crime, the reporters (conflating the term *terrorist* with Arab) could not read the massive Oklahoma bombing as a terrorist act. Despite the magnitude of the Oklahoma bombing, this statement implies it can only be labeled an act of terror if Arabs are to blame.

Indeed, political cartoons also reveal society's desperate need to incriminate the Arab "other." A cartoon in the *New York Post* on April 21, 1995, depicted three turbaned men, one of whom was holding a bomb, burning the American flag next to the Statue of Liberty. The inscription on the statue read, "Give us your tired, your poor, your huddled masses, your terrorists, your murderers, your slime, your evil cowards, your religious fanatics . . ." (*ADC Times* 1995, 4). The terms *religious fanatics* and *terrorists* are metonyms for Middle Eastern people, and the obvious caricaturing of Arab men enables this cartoon to play on racist cultural assumptions regarding Arabs without directly naming them. The iconography of the Statue of Liberty suggests the site in which the "other" ideally becomes American. This cartoon implies that the Middle Eastern immigrant, however, is not only incapable of being a "real" American, but also actually intends to harm the American people. The Arab men burning the American flag—a symbol of America's people, values, and way of life— echoes President Clinton's thinly veiled Orientalist statement. The symbolic speech of the cartoon depicts Arabs/Arab Americans as antithetical to who "we" are, thus implying that they pose a threat to "our" way of life.

This cartoon goes far beyond implicating Arabs in the Oklahoma bombing, for it effectively slanders the character of all Arabs, including the 2.5 million American citizens of Arab descent currently living in the United States. The indirect message is that regardless of their American citizenship, Arabs should never be trusted as fellow Americans. In the event of a large-scale attack directed at Americans, this cartoon reinforces that the first inclination of guilt should be toward Arabs, who were referred to by one talk-show host as "heathen savages [from] Towelhead nations" (Grunwald 1995, 28).

Not surprisingly, several talk-radio hosts spewed hate messages in the wake of the bombing, often defaming Arabs and Muslims as "rag heads." Hate speech—whether hidden in the "objective" language of terrorist experts, implied in the political rhetoric of the government, or made explicit in the vile words of talk radio—creates a climate of acceptable racism. "Violence," as one legal scholar cogently argues, "is a necessary and inevitable part of racism. It is the final solution, as fascists know, barely held at bay while the tactical weapons of segregation, disparagement, and hate propaganda do this work" (Matsuda et al. 1993, 24).

During the Gulf War, evidence of the repercussions of hate speech was plentiful. "The 1991 Report on Anti-Arab Hate Crimes" chronicles incidents of political and hate violence directed at Arab Americans from January to August 1991.[2] Because of the intimidation that members of Arab American communities experienced, this document does not nearly represent the extent of crimes committed against Arab Americans during the period. According to the

hate-crimes document, Arab Americans were "the target of FBI and other of-
ficial investigations," based solely on their ethnicity (Eiken and Gorchev 1992,
2). This creates a climate that presupposes the guilt of Arab Americans. It is no
wonder, then, that many Arab Americans were silenced in reporting acts of verbal and physical violence—feeling as if their treatment was legitimized by the
discourse of the mass-media culture and the government.

The media's dehumanization of Arabs as the "other" and the "enemy" in
large part enables anti-Arab hate crimes to occur. While these racist crimes
range from personalized verbal attacks to acts of physical brutality, they all con-
vey a message of otherness and often provoke violence. One notable example
is a popular T-shirt many Americans proudly wore during the Gulf War, which
featured an Arab man on a camel in the target sight of a rifle; the caption read,
"I'd fly 10,000 miles to smoke a camel." This T-shirt signifies American patriotism at the expense of Arab lives: Arabs are dehumanized as animals that
should be exterminated by the comparatively rational, superior Americans. Regardless of American citizenship, the binary of Arab and American that this
T-shirt's message reflects alienates Arab American citizens who, marked by
their ethnicity, were often labeled "terrorists" and "traitors" during the war.
They were harassed verbally and often told to "go home" or else suffer the consequences. While many of these threats were idle, a significant number of physical assaults, bombings, and the like accompanied death threats and intimidat-
ing words.

Racist invectives and physical assaults directed at Arab Americans during
the Gulf War provide a paradigm through which the myriad racist acts that followed the Oklahoma City bombing could have been predicted. Arab Americans
and Muslims reported hundreds of threats in the three days following the bombing. Many of the threats labeled Arabs as, among other things, "baby-killers"
and "animals." Mosques and homes were vandalized throughout the country,
effectively conveying the message of one caller to a talk-radio show who stated,
"You [Arabs] bring terror to this country . . . I want you out of here" (*ADC
Times* 1995, 1).

Abraham Ahmad, an American citizen originally from Jordan and a resi-
dent of Oklahoma City, was another victim of racial stereotyping. Shortly after
the bombing, Ahmad was detained before leaving the United States on his way
to visit his family in Jordan. He was held in Chicago for questioning by the
FBI, was released, and flew to London to catch a connecting flight to Jordan. In
London, he was detained again and forced to return to the United States for further interrogation by the FBI. Before he left, he was strip-searched and questioned by British authorities. Speculations about the "Middle Eastern" man with
"bomb-making equipment" in his luggage resounded through the press. The
media incriminated Ahmad and his family in Oklahoma suffered as a result. In
actuality, the "bomb-making equipment" consisted of items Ahmad was taking
to his family in Jordan: "a potato peeler, a skillet, knives, spoons, a VCR, and
other small appliances" (*ADC Times* 1995, 1). Ahmad, in a news conference,

reflected on his ordeal by stating, "I want the American public to understand that we are human beings, too, and it is not fair to just judge people by their color or origin . . ." (*ADC Times* 1995, 1).

Color and origin, however, remain primary determinants of narrative identification. The narratives attached to people of color are so stable that they appear to many as normative, not cultural productions at all. Racist mythologies reinforce the ideal of "white" supremacy by scapegoating members of ethnic groups as morally inferior. Salam Al Marayati of the Muslim Public Affairs Council concretizes some prevalent ethnic narratives: "Every Muslim becomes a potential terrorist. Every African American is a potential gangbanger. Every Latino is a potential illegal immigrant. It's bias that is used against us" (Quintanilla 1995, E1). It is evident that Susan Smith, for example, the South Carolina woman who claimed that an African American man abducted her children, was familiar with these narratives. She was banking on the efficacy of racist mythology to deflect attention away from herself. For a period she was successful, as the country desperately searched for this fictitious man and her two children—interrogating innocent African American men along the way.

In both of these cases, the rush to judgment underscores the ease with which culpability is placed on the ethnic other. However, the import of these incidents lies in the disruption of racial sensibilities. The demonizing rhetoric portraying Arabs as "Muslim extremists" and "terrorists" laid the foundation for Americans' assumption that Arabs committed this deadly act of terrorism. However, when the pictures of the two suspects were shown, America's narrative of good and evil was shaken: the men appeared to be "white." Later reports confirmed that Timothy McVeigh and Terry Nichols, two Euro-American men who had served in the U.S. Armed Forces, were formally charged with the crime. Despite this fact, several terrorist experts persisted in connecting the horror to the Middle East. The media circulated the idea—again, in the absence of fact—that perhaps McVeigh was merely a pawn in an international (read Middle Eastern) game of terror, thus revealing the country's inability to dispose of racist mythology. Newspaper articles with captions that read "Many Jarred at Finding Suspect Is an American" and "A Shocked America Finds Enemy Within" reveal the overall disbelief that Americans—especially Euro-Americans—could be capable of such evil.

Considering the outright vilification of Arab Americans and Muslims by mainstream American society, the larger group of marginalized people would seem to offer refuge. Recognizing the commonalties of people of color, marginalized people have joined voices to create communities of strength, solidarity, and celebration. The diverse members of this community are linked by a common history of oppression and misrepresentation. In critiquing their representation in dominant media/popular culture (out of which social constructions are born), this community has addressed its marginalization through exposure, analysis, and critique. However, when "Middle Eastern" people turn to this site of healing, they are often remarginalized and cast within the same Orientalist

narrative. Because of our absence in multi-ethnic anthologies and classes purporting to represent diverse populations, for example, and the seeming disregard to remedy this exclusion on the part of other people of color, one scholar
has aptly labeled Arab Americans "The Most Invisible of the Invisibles" (Kadi
1994, xix).

Arab American authors have done much to counter their societal invisibility and to question constructions of Arabs in mass media discourse. Naomi
Shihab Nye is exemplary of recent writers who challenge Orientalist rhetoric
in their work. "Marked" by her father as Arab American, she inevitably turns
to that paternal source as a way in which to understand and mediate her marginalized American cultural identity. In this way, Nye necessarily speaks the father as she speaks the self. Mapping her identity as an Arab American through
the body of her Palestinian father, Nye uses corporeal metaphors to underscore
her material connection to her father, the Middle East, and the Arab people.

Defining the Arab American female literary and material subject in terms
of the Arab father, Nye counters the omnipresent cultural narrative of Arab
male sexism and patriarchal violence. Nye recovers the beauty of her heritage
from the script of Western imperialism, and wrests the Arab female body from
Western inscription. Reading the (covered) woman's body/text as a site of Arab
male misogyny and brutality, the West inscribes her as a passive, obedient, silenced victim of patriarchy. Therefore, in using the metaphorics of the body in
her work, Nye liberates the Arab (and Arab American) woman's body and consequently that of the Arab male.

The domestic sphere functions as a trope of cultural resistance in Nye's
poetry: the home is articulated as a site of resistance, and domestic rituals are
identified as political acts. Shifting the ideological terrain of the home allows
Nye the space in which to negotiate a dialectic between public and private, Arab
and American, father and daughter, and body and text. Conceptualizing the domestic as a political arena, Nye addresses highly charged issues in understated,
seemingly apolitical verse. Gregory Orfalea, for example, acknowledges that
"The Man Who Makes Brooms" is one of Nye's best "protest" poems (1991,
58). In this piece, Nye pays tribute to the ritualized activity of a Palestinian
broom maker: "It is a song, this thumb over thumb, / but sometimes when you
wait years for the air to break open / and sense to fall out, / it may be the only
one" (27–31). The constancy of the ritual is in stark contrast to the displacement and exile of the community. For Nye, the broom maker's song assures a
kind of cultural permanency in a land that promises none. Nye pays tribute to
the man who makes brooms, recognizing that the space he occupies, regardless
of its diminutive size, is his own. Furthermore, his quiet occupation also provides a counter-text to the ingrained stereotype of the young, angry Palestinian
terrorist, a resonant narrative in the West. Nye infuses the broom, a domestic
object, with cultural meaning. When the speaker's uncle asks, "No brooms in
America?" (24), the trajectory of the poem is expanded to include the West,
again revealing the tension between the landscape of Nye's birth and the landscape of her heritage.

Despite the fact that Nye's work is not obviously political, her choices of writing autobiographical poetry signifies an attempt to contravene cultural scripts. As Sidonie Smith claims:

> autobiographical writing has played and continues to play a role in emancipatory politics. Autobiographical practices become occasions for restaging subjectivity, and autobiographical strategies become occasions for the staging of resistance . . . the autobiographer can lay out an agenda for a changed relationship to subjectivity, identity and the body. (1993, 156–157)

Speaking the silenced body of an Arab American woman and constructing that subjectivity in relationship to her father, Nye in fact writes subversively political poetry.

The aptly titled poem "Blood" exemplifies Nye's articulation of identity, as the identifiable self of the poems is the collective "I" of father and daughter. The title refers to familial bloodlines while at the same time signifying racial violence. The speaker of the poem is Nye herself, illustrated by the discussion of her familial surname. The poem has an Arabic folkloric quality, as the speaker's father instructs his young daughter about what a "true Arab" does and believes. The father's lessons range from how "true Arabs" can catch flies in their hands and use watermelon for medicinal purposes, to how "true Arabs" love and revere nature. The beginning of the poem appears apolitical, as the father merely relays to his daughter her cultural heritage in an innocuous manner. While there is no overt discussion of the political nature of being Arab in America, the child soon learns the ramifications of that identification in the West.

In the third stanza Nye writes, "years before, a girl knocked, / wanted to see the Arab. / I said we didn't have one" (8–10). The young visitor, while not occupying a place of power in their lives, does in fact bring societal narratives into the interior domain of the home. The young Nye of the poem may not understand the complexity of the child's query, but she apprehends that otherness is being enacted at that moment as the public and private geographies of her life collide. Nye continues that stanza with "After that, my father told me who he was, / "Shihab"—shooting star—/ a good name, borrowed from the sky. / Once I said, 'When we die we give it back?' / He said that's what a true Arab would say" (11–15). This stanza exemplifies the state of double consciousness that so many people of color experience. Nye's choice of the words "after that" implies that the young girl's father recognizes the social narratives that will become omnipresent in his daughter's life and his responsibility to provide a counter-script for this racism. By telling his daughter the meaning of their name—"who he was"—he enables Nye to come to know and identify with her rich heritage.

Labeling his daughter a "true Arab" in this third stanza becomes a critical moment of transition, for the seriousness of assuming that identity in America is concretized in the rest of the poem. The last two stanzas underscore the family's struggle to apprehend its cultural alienation. The media is again implicated in the family's pain: "Today the headlines clot in my blood" (16). Not only are the speaker and her father traumatized by the brutality occurring in their homeland, but the media's biased representation of this crisis furthers the violence.

Voices of father and daughter commingle in "Blood" to create an alternative cultural text. With a keen understanding of how the Arab male has been discursively created as an American scapegoat, Nye rescues her father—the Arab father—from cultural misrepresentation. Establishing that language is a critical space from which to work, Nye's poetry *is* a site of resistance: it ruptures racist stereotypes and speaks the "true Arab" self. Expanding the cultural scope of Arab identity, Nye's is a significant voice denouncing the continued construction and perpetuation of the "other."

Notes

1. Pressure from the American-Arab Anti-Discrimination Committee (ADC), an organization dedicated to defending the rights of Arab Americans, forced the Disney Corporation to change some of the more blatantly racist lyrics for the home-video release.

2. In compiling the material for this report, ADC used the United States Justice Department guidelines on hate-crime data collection. This document does not, then, include racist products nor anti-Arab/anti-Muslim remarks made by the media.

Works Cited

ADC. 1995. "Oklahoma Tragedy Highlights Bias Against Arab Americans." *ADC Times.* 16.2: 1+.

ADC. 1995. *Oklahoma City Bombing: Preliminary Report on Anti-Arab/Muslim Harassment.* Washington, DC: ADC Research Institute, 1995.

Barthes, Roland. 1957. *Mythologies.* Trans. Annette Lavers. New York: Noonday.

Benedetto, Richard. 1995. "For Clinton, a Chance to Unify, to Take Charge." *USA Today.* 21 April 1995: 3A.

Eiken, Larry, and Leila Gorchev (eds.). 1992. *1991 Report on Anti-Arab Hate Crimes: Political and Hate Violence against Arab-Americans.* Washington, DC: ADC Research Institute.

Grunwald, Michael. 1995. "Muslims Fear Being Made Scapegoats." *Boston Globe.* 21 April 1995: 1+.

Kadi, Joanna (ed.). 1994. "Introduction." *Food for Our Grandmothers: Writings by Arab-Americans and Arab-Canadian Feminists.* Boston: South End Press. xiii–xx.

Lubiano, Wahneema. 1992. "Black Ladies, Welfare Queens, and State Justice: Ideological War by Narrative Means." *Race-ing Justice, En-gendering Power.* Ed. Toni Morrison. New York: Pantheon. 323–363.

Matsuda, Mari J., et al. 1993. *Words That Wound: Critical Race Theory, Assaultive Speech, and the First Amendment.* San Francisco: Westview.

Michalak, Laurence. 1988. *Cruel and Unusual: Negative Images of Arabs in American Popular Culture.* 3rd Ed. Washington, DC: ADC Research Institute.

Not Without My Daughter. Directed by Brian Gilbert. 1990.

Nye, Naomi Shihab. 1995. "Blood." *Words Under the Words.* Portland: Eighth Mountain Press. 121.

———. 1995. "The Man Who Makes Brooms." *Words Under the Words.* Portland: Eighth Mountain Press. 127.

Orfalea, Gregory. 1991. "Doomed by Our Blood to Care: The Poetry of Naomi Shihab Nye." *Paintbrush.* Spring. 56–66.

Quinn-Judge, Paul, and Charles M. Sennott. "Specialists Say the Attack Marks Turning Point in US." *Boston Globe.* 20 April 1995: A24.

Quintanilla, Michael. 1995. "Divided We Stand." *Los Angeles Times.* 28 April 1995: E3+.

Said, Edward J. 1978. *Orientalism.* New York: Vintage.

Shammas, Anton. 1995. "Presumed Guilty." *The New York Times.* 4 May 1995: A25.

Sharif, Michelle. 1994. "Global Sisterhood: Where Do We Fit In?" *Food for Our Grandmothers: Writings by Arab-Americans and Arab-Canadian Feminists.* Ed. Joanna Kadi. Boston: South End Press. 151–159.

Smith, Sidonie. 1993. *Subjectivity, Identity and the Body.* Bloomington: Indiana University Press.

Zaldivar, R.A., and Steve Goldstein. 1995. "Experts Say It's Too Early to Assign Blame for Blast on Any One Group." *The Philadelphia Inquirer.* 20 April 1995: A23.

4

Higher Learning: Composition's Racialized Reflection

Keith Gilyard

In John Singleton's 1993 film *Higher Learning,* central character Malik Williams is bombarded with racist imagery from the moment he steps onto the campus of Columbus University. Under cloak of the American flag—the movie's opening shot features Old Glory—all sorts of stereotyping and racialized discourse play out. White students make snide remarks about Mexicans on scholarship. Authorities suppress African American cultural expression. A woman of European extraction clutches her bag when alone in an elevator with Malik. Nothing is subtle in this collage of racialized metaphors and ironies. In fact, Malik is himself, at first blush, a stereotype. On a track scholarship, he is the black athlete who has literally run his way into college.

During Malik's first semester, he enrolls in Political Science 101 taught by Professor Maurice Phipps, who is either clumsily trying reverse psychology or is an arrogant and pompous poster boy for African American neoconservativeness. When Malik asserts, "I ain't no dumb athlete," Phipps unsupportively suggests that the question remains to be resolved.

Fudge, a sort of spiritual leader among African American students at Columbus, pushes Malik further on issues of intellect and identity. At a social gathering, he quizzes Malik about his purpose for attending college, his aspirations and expectations. Fudge is disappointed because Malik expresses an interest only in making "that long dough," not in political activism or the pursuit of useful knowledge. Seeking to test the degree of Malik's conformity, Fudge solicits Malik's response to a hypothetical situation in which Malik is the only African American in an otherwise white audience at a football game; the national anthem is about to be played and all eyes turn to Malik, who is seated directly below the American flag. Malik confesses that, mostly out of embarrassment, he would stand along with the rest of the crowd. Fudge is despaired by the answer because he wants to elicit commentary indicative of the need for protest, but he quickly realizes that he is not talking to anyone like Mahmoud Abdul-Rauof, the former Denver Nuggets star who became the center of controversy when he refused to stand for the Pledge of Allegiance at several games during the 1995–1996 NBA season. Softening his tone somewhat, Fudge inquires:

> "So they got you runnin' for the school, hunh?"
> "Yeah. Partial scholarship."
> "And if you don't run you don't get no tuition, right?"
> "That's the way the system goes."
> "Run nigger run."

Fudge makes this last reply in resignation, expressing dismay that Malik is unaware that, in Fudge's view, he is being exploited.

On another occasion, this time at Fudge's place, Malik asks to borrow a copy of one of the autobiographies of Frederick Douglass. Amazed by the number of books on Fudge's shelves, he asks if Fudge, indeed, reads them all. Fudge assures Malik that he reads most of them. Furthermore, he is excited by the prospect that Malik has chosen to absorb Douglass' powerful rhetoric as part of a program to educate himself. His mood changes, though, when Malik concedes that he needs the book for class and, in fact, can conceive of no other reason to peruse it. Fudge ushers Malik to the door with the admonition to "read it for yourself and not no damn class."

The dialogues among Professor Phipps, Malik, and Fudge initiate a series of related encounters within the racialized arena that is Columbus University and also open onto conversations—most important here—about paper assignments in such a setting. Phipps assigns a research paper or term project that requires students to form and express their own political ideologies, which he says will come out of each student's "sex, background, social and economic status, personal experiences, etc., etc." Many compositionists, particularly those of a postmodern persuasion, easily detect the contradictions inherent in the assignment. Students are being asked for their subjective ideologies at the same time that they are encouraged to play a rather crude form of identity politics (exactly how crude depends on what terms like *come out of* and *background* mean precisely). Notwithstanding, students generate writing over the course of the semester, geared presumably toward realizing the stated goal. On the first paper, Malik receives a B for content and a C for form. Indignant, he approaches Professor Phipps at the front of the classroom and is informed that the disappointing grade was given because of numerous grammar, spelling, and punctuation errors. During the ensuing dialogue, which is largely unproductive—at one point Malik terms his teacher a "sellout"—Professor Phipps rejects the notion that any of Williams' problems stem from racism. He argues, instead, that Malik's problems are a function of class, not racism, and are therefore temporary.

Malik's counter-contention—and he is right both in the context of the film and as related to most of the academic world beyond—is that racism is part of the basic fiber of the university and that perhaps professors like Phipps have some proactive role to play in combating it. However, Phipps generally refuses to engage Malik's view of the world or the content of his papers. He merely offers the opinion that black people are primarily disfranchised because of their own laziness and reminds Malik that he, one Professor Phipps, did not ask Malik to come to the university in the first place. The very next shot is of "lazy" black athletes running and jumping, representing the university at a track meet.

For help with his writing assignments, Malik turns to his girlfriend Deja; her pedagogy, and his response to it, echo what we have heard many times in writing centers across the nation:

> "Run-on, run-on, fragment, fragment, fragment. Is this supposed to be a period or a comma?"
> "It's a whole lot of red ink."
> "Do you want help?"
> "I'm here."
> "Look, you gotta get this to flow and right now it's not flowing. Okay, look right here. That's a good point, but you gotta follow it up with a concise explanation."
> "What you mean?"
> "Malik, when you write a essay you gotta follow a certain format. You start with a thesis statement. And always use transitional phrases. And don't use the same word every single time. Change it up, you know? Professors hate that. Use a thesaurus. And where's your outline?"
> "Hunh?"
> "You gotta lot of work to do."

Malik indeed does work, submitting an improved product the next time around, which results, unfortunately, in Phipps questioning the essay's authorship. Malik feistily asserts that he wrote the paper and was fairly certain it contained no misspellings. Phipps capitulates, his chiding perhaps having been a well-meaning ploy. Telling, though, is that he offers no comments about the paper's content.

By this point in the film, or in this essay, self-styled progressive composition instructors perhaps have become somewhat smug, even cynical, with regard to Professor Phipps and the manner in which he deals with texts. Although not a writing instructor, he commands a site of textual production and is in a position to influence the development of writing. In fact, because there may be more interest on the part of students in his subject matter than in composition, he may be in a more influential position than most composition instructors. Therefore, his practice needs drastic improvement; he needs to be put through the paces at CCCC, some Writing Across the Curriculum initiative, or an appropriate summer institute so he would cease committing egregious errors in pedagogy. He would learn that an instructor should respond fully to student work, tactfully so, and in as private a space as possible. He would discontinue his penchant for cavalierly dismissing papers because of punctuation errors and then, having browbeaten the student writer about correctness, questioning the integrity of the writer relative to subsequent submissions. It does not appear, however, that compositionists can be as smug about Professor Phipps' other major shortcoming—that is, the failure to comprehend more fully, and the subsequent inability to address effectively, the racialized or racially inscribed atmosphere of the university. Are we confident that we as teachers respond most logically to racialized realities, especially along the axis of language, our stock in trade? Maybe not.

Even as our profession largely converted to multiculturalism in the 1980s, an advent that is connected to though not synonymous with the political turn in composition studies noted by some (see Wiley 1996, 417–423), it was apparent that composition instructors as a whole had not confronted deeply enough issues of race, racism, and racialized discourse. Although challenges to racism and exclusion launched the multicultural movement, the rhetoric and aims of that movement are not necessarily coterminous with the rhetoric and aims of, say, anti-racism. While the former often gestures toward a formulaic polycultural curriculum, the latter insists on unflinching criticism of racist domination and its impact on education, including composition curricula. Multiculturalism, then, with its characteristic emphasis on rather low-level sensitivity training, serves to obscure the problematics of racism, which (Phipps notwithstanding) include consideration of class.

Part of what accounts for the divergence between multicultural and antiracist agendas is the notion of race itself. For some it is a biological, in fact, objective term that signifies an ultimately defining complex of naturally occurring differences. It is, in short, reified. Such reification of race leads some down predictable rhetorical paths: pleas for racial harmony and interracial cooperation. This explains many of the paeans to multiculturalism that have been a major feature of composition conferences and publications for the past decade. Insufficiently acknowledged is that race is at least partly a social and rhetorical construction. Some even argue that it is all social and rhetorical construction, especially in the mongrelized American context, a position numerous biologists and anthropologists would support.

This sets up a different line of inquiry. How, for instance, do the socially constructed "races" of teachers and students make a difference in writing classrooms? More to the point, if race is not objectively real, or at least unreal in part, then appeals for multiracial tolerance—which are at the heart of multicultural discourse by composition instructors—become diminished in relevance if not altogether immaterial. Obviously, the existence of "multi-races" logically has to precede a call for multiracial tolerance and cooperation. If so-called races are not naturally at odds, or are not natural at all, then a call for multiracial tolerance is not a solution for a natural problem. Nor is is it necessarily the solution for a socially constructed one. Where do compositionists, then, find a better line to push about race? One might expect direction from a cultural-studies or critical-discourse wing of the profession, and there has been some, albeit not entirely clear.

The late James Berlin, in "Composition and Cultural Studies," argues for making students aware of controlling discourses (1991, 50). Describing a course that merges methods of composition studies and cultural studies, he writes that:

> The focus is on the relation of current signifying practices to the structuring of subjectivities—of race, class, and gender formations, for example—in our students and ourselves. Our effort is to make students aware of the cultural codes—the various competing discourses—that attempt to influence who they are. Our larger purpose is to encourage our students to resist and to negotiate these codes—these hegemonic discourses—in order to bring about more personally humane and socially equitable economic and political arrangements. (50)

However, neither in this essay nor in subsequent work does Berlin get around to explaining the controlling, hegemonic discourse that "race" is. I do not intend this to be a harsh criticism. Berlin was certainly aware of the limitations of both his theorizing and his courses; he remarked so explicitly in the "Into the Classroom" chapter of his final book, *Rhetoric, Poetics, and Cultures* (1996, 115). And this is not to dispute his commitment to liberatory pedagogy; such would be foolish. I merely aim to point out that if a rhetorician as critically sensitive and astute as Berlin, who was obsessed with how cultural codes implicitly operate, failed to crack the "race" code for us, it is strong testimony to how potently invisible, or invisibly potent, that particular code signifies. Furthermore, because rhetoric is inherently ideological, as Berlin himself declared, he compromised his own teaching project by not attending to the issue of "race" more critically. From the subject position of a white teacher, a label he did not reject, how could he teach students to "resist" and "negotiate" the controlling discourse that "whiteness" is?

I do not argue that this kind of clarity on "race" is indispensable—although I obviously feel it quite valuable—to teaching and writing. But because a tremendous amount of time is consumed in composition classrooms discussing issues of "race," it almost goes without saying that this talk should clarify as opposed to obfuscate. The case in most classrooms, though, is that "race" simply inscribes another othering discourse. It is an unproblematized marker of the nonwhite, the other. Imagine a large group of Euro-Americans deciding to discuss the issue of race and then focusing the discussion on themselves and how they have been constructed racially. I would wager that this rarely happens among Euro-Americans, but this is precisely the move that has to occur repeatedly if the liberatory curriculum is to be realized to its greatest possibility. Casting race analysis in conventional terms leads students to pedestrian interpretations and constructions inside a bankrupt race-relations model, thus leading to a sort of King to King solution, students dreaming and all getting along—rhetorically.

Providing necessary emendation for the likes of Berlin, American Studies instructor Ruth Frankenburg (1993) articulates how "whiteness" operates as a dominating nexus of constructs. She argues that:

> Examining the construction of whiteness and other racial identities is useful because it may help lead white activists (and also, for that matter, activists of color) away from the incorporation of "old" discursive elements into "new" strategies. I have, for example, argued that we need to displace the colonial construction of whiteness as an "empty" cultural space, in part by refiguring it as constructed and dominant rather than as norm. Without reconceptualizing culture, we run the risk of reifying and dehistoricizing *all* cultural practices, valorizing or romanticizing some while discounting others as not cultural at all. But a dualistic framework is retained, for example, in new curricular programs that include attention to nondominant cultures but do not simultaneously reconceptualize or reexamine the status, content, and formation of whiteness. (242–243)

Inside composition studies, or perhaps college English more broadly, Ann-Louise Keating (1995) has recently voiced similar concerns. Her own courses interrogate the construction of racialized identities, sometimes to the bewilderment of her students for whom such framing of thought appears quite strange. Keating notes that although her students can rather easily pursue the question of racialized themes in relation to works by Leslie Marmon Silko, N. Scott Momaday, Paula Gunn Allen, Nella Larsen, and Paul Laurence Dunbar, they are stumped when asked to perform the same task with respect to the writing of Joanna Russ, John Updike, Ralph Waldo Emerson, and Henry David Thoreau. Their consternation reaffirms for me the efficacy of activity, like Keating's and Frankenberg's, that seeks to (de)construct "race." Not to do so, in the contexts in which we work, is to confirm the prevailing discourse and to be implicated in the maintenance of an exploitative social order to the exact extent that said discourse promotes exploitation.

What is the source, then, of a narrative about racial formation that would be useful in composition classrooms, one accessible yet sufficient in scope? To place first things first, we have to turn, of course, to history. As Roger Sanjek (1994) writes:

> Race is the framework of ranked categories segmenting the human population that was developed by western Europeans following their global expansion beginning in the 1400s. . . . The labels used in race ranking—"Negro," "Indian," "white," "mulatto," "half-caste," "Oriental," "Alpine," "Aborigine"— have varied in number, currency, assumed precision, and acceptability over

time. The underlying scales of imputed racial quanta of intelligence, attractiveness, cultural potential, and worth have varied hardly at all. To contemporary anthropologists, none of this scaling is "real," though it has been real enough in its effects. Race has become all too real in its social ordering of perceptions and policies, in the perverse racism that has plagued the globe following the 1400s. For worse, not better, we all live in a racialized world. (1)

"Race," then, was an ideology developed in the interests of imperialists and continued to function as rationalization for continuing systems of oppression. That people enjoy privilege at the expense of those they naturally "outrank" was presumed to be understandable. The relevant taxonomy, however, had to be developed over time. At the outset of enslavement in the colonies, there was no widespread belief by Europeans that all Europeans "outranked" all Africans. It would have been a hard posture to adopt for European indentured servants, who were sometimes aware of the presence of free Africans. The economic interests of indentured servants were more closely aligned with those of enslaved Africans than any other segment of the population; in fact, there were instances, such as Bacon's Rebellion in 1676, where joint demands were made to end bond labor. The problem for the ruling class, then, was how to separate the aspirations of indentured servants, whose term of bondage was finite, from those of the enslaved, who were to be (if all worked in favor of the masters) suppressed in perpetuity. The solution is described by Theodore Allen (1994):

> Since the poor European-Americans were or, after a term of servitude, would be free, and since they typically had already lost upward social mobility, they were promoted to the "white race" and endowed with unprecedented civil and social privileges, vis-a-vis the African American, privileges that, furthermore, were made to appear to be conditional on keeping "not-whites" down and out. This entailed the exclusion of "free Negroes" from participation in the buffer role in the continental colonies, because their inclusion would have undermined the racial privileges upon which depended the loyalty of the laboring-class "whites" to the plantation bourgeoisie. Whatever may have been the case with the literate members of the ruling class, the record indicates that laboring-class European-Americans in the continental plantation colonies showed little interest in "white identity" before the institution of the system of "race" privileges at the end of the seventeenth century. (14)

The rich, landed class, therefore, held a free class of not-too-happy Europeans, an increasing population of enslaved Africans, and a wary group of free Africans all in check by creating "whiteness." Put another way, "race" was the deal cut between working-class Europeans and the European bourgeoisie to ensure control of enslaved African labor. A little land, limited employment, certain civic access—in short, white-skin privilege—were swapped for commitment to overt social control along racial lines. "Whiteness" also has served to discourage the formation of class consciousness in other regions of the country as well, and among subsequent waves of European immigrants, who received their "promotions" upon arrival on these shores. Conversely, immigrants of color often have been, sometimes to their surprise, demoted in status. Indeed "race" has been used to discourage class consciousness among all groups. The main point for these purposes, though, is that everyone in the United States has a default identity relative to whiteness formation, which was in itself a carefully calculated social maneuver. Refusal to embrace the prescription constitutes both choice and statement and would be a move by composition teachers and students—a shift away from "white" teachers and "white" students—consistent with though not immediately assumable from goals described by theorists like Berlin.

Now I can already hear, or have heard, some of the objections to the position I take. "Oh, he's saying it's all about language." "He's saying that race is merely rhetorical and that just can't be true." "He is trying to minimize color differences and say that we're all the same." "He's trying to undermine a sense of community among African Americans." "He's saying I am racist if I identify myself as 'white,' but my ancestors are from several nations, including some partly in Asia, and 'Euro-American' just isn't an accurate designation for me." Let me assert clearly, therefore, that I am not saying those things. I have flirted with—but not argued—the line that language determines all action. Although ideology is embedded in discourses, any one of us is processing a multiplicity of discourses that influence our behaviors. It is entirely possible that racist verbal constructs are directly responsible for racist actions, but it is also possible for one to act humanely even while operating inside a certain language of inhumanity. What one cannot do, however, when locked inside the discourse of "race" is to show the way out of that position. Thus, one is implicated to the degree that that discourse is delimiting. The "degree" is what we need to investigate further and continue to do so deeply and frequently. Moreover, although I have posited that race is rhetorical, I have not suggested that it is *merely* so. It does become its various significations and is, as pointed out by Sanjek, real in its effects. I, for one, have always known the law: If the gun is empty, I still get the armed-robbery charge, even if I'm armed only with rhetorical bullets. Likewise, Deja, who is killed by a neo-Nazi terrorist, suffers more than a socially constructed death, and the racial slights that Malik experiences are real despite the fact that he—and Professor Phipps, for that matter—cannot articulate them fully. If current perception counts as much as historical reality, then why bother, one may ask, to make a fuss over distinctions and confuse the public? Because this essay is for academics who spend considerable amounts of time on "race" and presume to be educating students about the concept, not for lay persons who live out various racializations and with whom I would enter into a different dialogue.

I am not asserting that we are all the same regardless of color. While that may be true in the broadest sense, it would be nonsensical to deny that color and ethnicity make all kinds of difference in this nation. To deconstruct "race" is not to imply that everyone is the same, but rather to contribute to fuller explanations of the racialized disparities we see, a clarification that does not in itself work against the idea of African American solidarity. Group struggle by African Americans depends on how well culture and shared ideals bind us together, not on establishing an essential racial category. The issue is ideological, not biological, as most of the African American community well knows, which is why we have language—"sellout" (as Malik says), "handkerchief head," "oreo," "Uncle Tom," "Uncle Thomas, Ph.D.," even "Uncle Thomas, Supreme Court Justice"—to describe those seen as traitors to the common cause. The nature and relationship of that communal initiative—or even conceptions of what that initiative ought to be—and how such activity should connect to larger efforts toward social justice are matters that will be debated by members of the community, and always have been.

As for the last objection indicated previously, I trust it is evident that I do not believe that all self-described white persons are necessarily racist. I cannot name them as well as they would like. Perhaps that famous Cablinasian, Tiger Woods, can lend a hand. My project at this point is not to name but to unmask.

I assume, to be charitable, that Professor Phipps eventually will move his charges—though he won't do so well with their writing—toward some understanding that large social forces impact their ideological premises. If not, what good is his Political Science 101? I also assume that composition instructors—especially those who speak often of diversity and of getting students to understand, manipulate, or resist dominant discourses—will want to urge students to begin writing themselves outside the prevailing discourse on race.

Works Cited

Allen, Theodore. 1994. *The Invention of the White Race, Volume One: Racial Oppression and Social Control.* New York: Verso.

Berlin, James. 1996. *Rhetoric, Poetics, and Cultures.* Urbana, IL: National Council of Teachers of English.

———. 1991. "Composition and Cultural Studies." *Composition and Resistance.* Eds. C. Mark Hurlbert and Michael Blitz. Portsmouth, NH: Boynton/Cook. 47–55.

Frankenburg, Ruth. 1993. *White Women, Race Matters: The Social Construction of Whiteness.* Minneapolis: University of Minnesota Press.

Higher Learning. 1993. Directed by John Singleton.

Keating, AnnLouise. 1995. "Interrogating 'Whiteness,' (De)Constructing 'Race'." *College English.* 57: 901–918.

Sanjek, Roger. 1994. "The Enduring Inequalities of Race." *Race.* Eds. Steven Gregory and Roger Sanjek. New Brunswick, NJ: Rutgers University Press. 1–17.

Wiley, Mark. 1996. "The (Re)Turn to the Political." *Composition in Four Keys: Inquiring into the Field.* Eds. Mark Wiley, Barbara Gleason, and Louise Wetherbee Phelps. Mountain View, CA: Mayfield. 417–423.

5

Fighting Back by *Writing* Black: Beyond Racially Reductive Composition Theory

David G. Holmes

For the most part, composition theory addressing the needs of African American students remains in the same state as African American literary studies during the 1960s. Composition theory on this subject still seemingly accepts the validity of reductive racial boundaries (specifically, the links among "race," dialect, and being), which the leaders of the Black Arts Movement reified.[1] This is particularly troubling since composition rhetoric often has emphasized tentative community and functional truth. The purpose of this essay, therefore, is to introduce the notion of race as rhetoric, or as a way of writing. My central argument is that in order for black voice to be most effective, the rhetoric of race itself must be recognized. In other words, the rhetor must use "blackness," instead of being used by it. The move, then, is from *black* writing to *writing* black.

Before introducing this idea, however, I will briefly discuss the construction of authorship during the Black Arts Movement, how other African Americans eventually countered this movement, and the preliminary implications for current composition pedagogy.

From the Black Arts Movement to the New Black Aesthetic

The Black Arts Movement, which lasted from the 1960s through the 1970s, was the second major African American literary movement. It was decidedly more political than the Harlem Renaissance. In fact, the Black Arts Movement was largely an outgrowth of the protest expressed by Richard Wright in the

1930s and 1940s. For Wright, social protest was the primary purpose for black art, and he felt that the need for that impulse would end when racism did. Wright's early collection of short stories, *Uncle Tom's Children;* magnum opus, *Native Son;* and autobiography, *Black Boy,* all confront the oppression and inhumane practices leveled against blacks.

Similarly, the Black Arts Movement addressed the need for long-awaited social equality for African Americans. These were the days of boycotts, sit-ins, freedom rides, student demonstrations, martyred civil-rights leaders, and broken promises—the days for passionate spokespersons: Martin Luther King, Jr., Malcolm X, Angela Davis, and Huey Newton, to name a few. Thus, the leaders of the Black Arts Movement longed to give voice to the struggles, hopes, and joys of the black masses; to legitimize through art their language, music, rituals, traditions, and informal everyday practices. It is to be expected, then, that during the Black Arts Movement, writers would more likely embrace as their role model the revolutionary shouting for her rights on the street corner rather than the poet contemplating in the woods. One of the leaders of this movement, Larry Neal, articulates this sentiment in a 1994 essay:

> The Black Arts Movement is radically opposed to any concept of the artist that alienates him from his community. Black Art is the aesthetic and spiritual sister of the Black Power concept. As such, it envisions an art that speaks directly to the needs and aspirations of Black America. In order to perform this task, the Black Arts Movement proposes a radical reordering of the western cultural aesthetic. It proposes a separate symbolism, mythology, critique, and iconology. The Black Arts and Black Power concept relate broadly to the Afro-American's desire for self-determination and nationhood. Both concepts are nationalistic. One is concerned with the relationship between art and politics; the other with the art of politics. (184)

To be sure, the image of the revolutionary artist can be useful. That is to say, sometimes it is legitimate—even desirable—for art to serve a social function. However, a problem with the Black Arts Movement was the way in which racial propaganda delimited the identity of the African American artist. In short, the question is this: Who should be the arbiter of authentic black identity and art?

Barbara Christian deems this issue important enough to introduce it into postmodern discussions of literary theory. For Christian, the deifying of postmodern literary theory devalues primary texts in that the contemporary scholar feels more obligated to analyze what other critics have said about texts than what authors themselves say through their imaginative writing. And in the postmodern move to open up primary texts to multiple readings, an elitism has evolved in which certain texts, many written by African Americans, never received close readings in the "traditional" sense.

This trend leads Christian to a critique of postmodern theory, not for the myriad questions provoked by its introduction into the academy, but for the "prescriptiveness" that, in many cases, has resulted from its uninhibited reign. In other words, the freedom represented by semantic indeterminacy and endless signifiers paradoxically enslaves one to a kind of reading that, by definition, must proscribe any reading that assumes meaning can be found. Curiously, Christian feels that the Black Arts Movement fell into this trap as well:

> I am particularly perturbed by the movement to exalt theory, as well, because of my own adult history. I was an active member of the Black Arts Movement in the 1960s and know how dangerous theory can become. Many today are not aware of this, but the Black Arts Movement tried to create a Black Literary Theory and in doing so became prescriptive. My fear is that when Theory is not rooted in practice, it becomes prescriptive, exclusive, and elitist.
>
> An example of this prescriptiveness is the approach the Black Arts Movement took towards language. For it, blackness resided in the use of black talk which they defined as hip urban language. So that when Nikki Giovanni reviewed Paule Marshall's *Chosen Place, Timeless People,* she criticized the novel on the grounds it wasn't black, for the language was too elegant, too white. Blacks, she said, did not speak that way. Having come from the West Indies where we do, some of the time, speak that way, I was amazed at the narrowness of her vision. The emphasis on *one* way to be black resulted in the works of Southern writers being seen as non-black since the black talk of Georgia does not sound like the black talk of Philadelphia. Because the ideologues, like Baraka, came from the urban centers, they tended to privilege their way of speaking, thinking, writing, and to condemn other kinds of writing as not black enough. . . . Older writers like Ralph Ellison and James Baldwin were condemned because they saw that the intersection of Western and African influences resulted in a new Afro-American culture. . . . (1994, 354–355)

Amiri Baraka (known as LeRoi Jones until 1967) played a major part in setting the tone for the Black Arts Movement. His play *Dutchman,* written in 1964 and that helped set the tone for the movement, denies the practicality of integration. And although Baraka produced books of poetry, plays, and a few collections of essays, the significance of his work for the evolution of African American literature pales in comparison to that of Ellison and Baldwin, who described the "intersection between Western and African influences" of which Christian speaks. Ellison, in particular, held to a dialectical take on black culture specifically and American culture generally. During the 1960s, he disagreed with those who rejected the melting pot as a metaphor for America. He saw this rejection as an attempt to dismiss the complexity of American identity. For him, the melting pot did not represent the loss of ethnic identity, therefore, but the tense yet essential interplay between minority cultures (and Ellison would include white culture within this definition) in the melding together of a new, American culture. Further, this mutual influencing (between whites and blacks, for instance) would exist regardless whether it was recognized by either group.

Likewise, James Baldwin's novels and essays complicate the distinctions among race, gender, and sexual orientation. Baldwin's sexual orientation contributed more to the Black Arts ideologues' rejection of his work than did his belief in the "intersection" between Western and African cultures. Baldwin was openly and proudly gay during a time when homosexuals were more oppressed than they are currently. And the homophobia that characterized black militant thinking during the 1960s was leveled against Baldwin in a number of ugly ways. At one point, for example, this socially conscious author was called "Martin Luther Queen."

The assumption that a few, in many cases sexist and homophobic, blacks were the arbiters of black identity and art led eventually to the emergence of the New Black Aesthetic. According to Henry Louis Gates, Jr. (1992), this movement questioned the borders of black identity posited during the Black Arts Movement. To some extent, the New Black Aesthetic mirrors "the range of representations of the meaning of blackness among the post-*Song of Solomon* (1978) era of black writers" (43). Trey Ellis clearly articulates the movement's thinking when he remarks: "The New Black Aesthetic says you have to *be* natural, you don't necessarily have to *wear* one" (Gates 1992, 145). Unlike their counterparts in the Black Arts Movement, Ellis and other proponents of this new aesthetic claim to be indifferent to what white people think (Gates 1992, 145). That is, their art is defined neither in terms of protest against nor in reverent imitation of mainstream discourse.

For Gates, the seminal texts for the New Black Aesthetic, or "points of the post-Black Aesthetic triangle," include Ellis' satire and manifesto "The New Black Aesthetic," Toni Morrison's cutting-edge attempt to transcend the "ultimate horror of black past—slavery" in her novel *Beloved,* and C. Eric Lincoln's effort to "preserve black vernacular culture for a younger generation" in his novel *The Avenue, Clayton City.* Notwithstanding the immense value of Morrison's and Lincoln's contributions to the formulation of the New Black Aesthetic, I am more interested in the satirical and parodic critique of Black Arts Movement essentialism. Like Ellis, George C. Woolfe wrote *The Colored Museum* in the 1980s to address the complexities of "black" identity. The following vignette from *The Colored Museum* illuminates the worth of this enterprise:

> But now let me tell you 'bout this function I went to the other night, way uptown. And baby when I say way uptown, I mean way-way-way-way-way-way-way-way uptown. Somewhere's between 125th Street and infinity.
>
> Inside was the largest gathering of black/Negro/colored Americans you'd ever want to see. Over in one corner you got Nat Turner sippin' champagne out of Eartha Kitt's slipper. And over in another corner, Bert Williams and Malcolm X was discussing existentialism as it relates to the shuffle-ball-change. Girl, Aunt Jemima and Angela Davis was in the kitchen sharing a plate of greens and just goin' off about South Africa. (1985, 50)

With this oversimplification, Woolfe chides efforts such as those enacted in the Black Arts Movement to conclusively define black culture. Woolfe juxtaposes opposite character types, time periods, and regions to highlight this absurdity. Bert Williams, one of the first black minstrels, would not be found in the company of Malcolm X, even if the two men were contemporaries, which they were not. The same holds true for Aunt Jemima and Angela Davis. Malcolm and Davis, active participants and—some would contend—icons of the Black Arts Movement, are paired with stereotypical images. The key to the passage, however, lies in Woolfe's conflating of "black/Negro/colored." The first designation is actually chronologically the last, and in conjoining them at the beginning of the passage, Woolfe sets the tone for the interchange between time, region, and character he discusses throughout the piece.

Woolfe and Ellis (as Gates argues) are heirs of Ishmael Reed's satire. Reed's *Mumbo Jumbo* was published in 1972 near the end of the Black Arts Movement. The book mocks the Western literary tradition, the Harlem Renaissance, and the Black Arts Movement, suggesting that academic, literary, and folk discourses are racialized. Reed, thereby, speaks to the ideological contexts of these literary traditions and exposes the rhetorics produced by them. He reveals a cultural communication gap between blacks and whites, based partly on the inability of whites to comprehend the essence of black language and literature, and partly on assumption by blacks that such an essence exists to begin with.[2]

Another way Reed shows the arbitrariness of academic discourse and literary traditions is to play with genre restrictions—the rhetoric of genre. Writers, in his view, should not be controlled by genre, but rather should control genre to accomplish their aims. Reed's book is a work of fiction, yet it contains footnotes and a partial bibliography. In the same manner, it defies arrangement. The book contains sections written in cursive, charts, and Chapter One begins before the title page and another page listing Reed's previous works. Most important, he criticizes the act of writing during the Harlem Renaissance and the Black Arts Movement by *writing*. The power is in the staging itself. This staging, according to Gates, also shapes the reading process:

> *Mumbo Jumbo*'s double narrative, then, its narrative-within-a-narrative, is an allegory of the act of reading itself. Reed uses this second mode of ironic omniscient narration to signify upon the nature of the novel in general but especially upon Afro-American naturalism and modernism. (Gates 1988, 229)

The leaders of the New Black Aesthetic have made an important move in questioning a narrow definition of sociopolitical and artistic voice among African Americans. However, these writers could have sufficiently strengthened their argument, which is really about black identity, by rigorously questioning what constitutes "blackness" itself. Woolfe, for example, destabilizes narrow race designations without attempting to transcend them. Still another essential step for the new black literati should have been to provide an alternative paradigm of authorship. It is helpful but insufficient to parody the folly of static designations of race and voice without discussing how these two concepts might be reconstructed while maintaining community.

The Students' Right to Their Own Language

Two years after *Mumbo Jumbo* was published in literary circles, *The Students' Right to Their Own Language* was published by the Conference on College Composition and Communication. The introduction emphasizes, among other matters, rhetoric and composition scholars' commitment to teaching a linguistically diverse student population:

> Differences in language have always existed, and the schools have always wrestled with them, but the social upheavals of the 1960s, and the insistence of submerged minorities on a greater share in American society have suggested the need for a shift in emphasis in providing answers. Should the schools try to uphold language variety, or to modify it, or to eradicate it? (Corbett 1974, 10)

Both the date when this document was written and the previous quote show how composition studies can be linked to the Black Arts and the New Black Aesthetic movements. By recognizing this "shift in emphasis," the writers of this document demonstrated their sensitivity to diverse social and academic concerns. Such sensitivity is, of course, in keeping with the rhetorical tradition of finding the social value of discourse. The question raised at the end of the previous paragraph seems to focus on the options available to writing teachers wishing to address linguistic diversity.

As one might expect, the document's design also reflects this sensitivity. A brief document, *The Students' Right to Their Own Language* poses and offers preliminary answers to fifteen questions that were and are socially, politically, and pedagogically relevant. These questions address issues such as defining dialect, determining the impact of dialect on the acquisition of literacy, and how adopting a liberal approach to linguistic diversity might affect the use of composition handbooks and standardized tests.

In other words, the document covers everything from fundamental definitions to more advanced implications. Indeed, postmodernists (who supposedly stress both sensitivity to and the endless pursuit of plurality) would applaud some of the observations made in the document. For example, like Michel Foucault, the writers of *The Students' Right to Their Own Language* consider knowledge—in this case, the privileging of Standard American English—the reflection of the hierarchy of power.

I too applaud the sensitivity to diversity represented in this document. In a few ways, however, it inadvertently creates the same shaky ideological foundation for composition pedagogy as the Black Arts Movement did for literary studies. For one thing, the existential investment students have in their respective dialects restricts pedagogical discussion. Accordingly, teachers are primarily responsible for cultivating the students' "self-esteem and self-image" by giving ample respect to their dialects.

And this is one of the places where *The Students' Right to Their Own Language* becomes confusing. Precisely, how are these various dialects to be honored? I ask this question in terms of purpose and pragmatics. One can establish the value of Black Dialect while emphasizing the rhetorical value of Standard American English. To teach Standard American English is not necessarily to denigrate Black Dialect. The issue that should have been stressed in this document is that Standard American English is a rhetorical strategy. To indict this marketplace dialect as merely the reflection of the current, oppressive power structure is to diminish its importance for the students' rhetorical repertoire.

If one cannot use the language of the marketplace, for whatever reason, then she is rhetorically disadvantaged. And this assessment is in no way an indictment of her own dialect. If Black Dialect were the language of the marketplace, then anyone who did not know how to use it would be rhetorically disadvantaged. But it isn't. Whether the language of the marketplace is influenced by dialects, may reflect disdain for those dialects, or reflects the dominant power structure are all immaterial to my point.

Moreover, the pedagogical benefits derived from dialect studies do not negate my contention. African American history is replete with individuals, from Frederick Douglass to Malcolm X, who saw the appropriation of mainstream literacy as one of the most effective means of articulating one's cultural values and defending oneself against the dominant culture.

I must reiterate that I am not minimizing the past or current pedagogical benefits of Black Dialect studies. It would be difficult to exaggerate what scholars such as Geneva Smitherman, William Labov, Shirley Brice Heath, Keith Gilyard, and a host of others have done to radically improve writing assessment. The purpose of this section, then, is not to categorically dismiss this body of scholarship. Rather, I intend to show how race as *a way of writing* can enhance these studies.

Black Vernacular and the Public Voice: The Limitations of Sociolinguistic Pedagogy

Kermit Campbell's *The Rhetoric of Black English Vernacular,* a doctoral dissertation written in 1993, calls for rethinking the role of vernacular in composition pedagogy. The following excerpt captures the essence of his project:

> . . . the key question in the literature has been whether African American children's failure to acquire or use standard written English is primarily due to linguistic differences or differences beyond language such as differences in culture. Although language and culture are hardly separable (and indeed we'll see that in some research one is but an extension of the other), the reported impact of each on students' acquisition and use of academic literacy varies from study to study. Thus, in what follows, I discuss linguistic and cultural differences as two generally opposing hypotheses. I then propose a third hypothesis which integrates language differences with differences in culture through a concept of BEV [Black English Vernacular] as rhetoric. (21)

Campbell intends "to describe the oral discourse practices of five African American male college students" (2). He argues, importantly, that some aspects of African American rhetoric are "embedded in students' academic prose" and considers the vernacular language of African Americans to be "central to an understanding of black verbal expression in most, if not *all* of its forms" (emphasis mine).

What is "black verbal expression" exactly? How encompassing is it, and what separates it from "white verbal expression?" If, by this term, he means the larger African American oral tradition, he should have made that point more clearly. Campbell acknowledges tacitly the problem of delineating rhetoric according to a static interpretation of race. For example, he places quotation marks around *"white,"* once when referring to white rhetoric.

The most compelling aspect of Campbell's study emerges when he recalls moments of personal interaction with the subjects for his study:

> The question I've quoted comes from an African American male student athlete who, during a tutoring session with me and other student athletes, had this reaction to some doubts raised about my cultural identity. The student who raised such doubts considered that although I was obviously black racially speaking, I was not black culturally speaking because I didn't talk like the "black brothers" who say "nigga." I found the occasion rather amusing at first, but, as I have pondered over it since then, the incident has come to symbolize for me the ambiguities of language and identity that mark the African American experience, including my own, within predominantly white universities. (54–55)

This passage resonates with my concern. That is, how do we move the students in our composition classrooms away from such presumption? Like Campbell, I have felt the tension between insider and outsider as I have taught African American students. Further, like Campbell, I feel "a relationship to the dialect as well as to the community of people who identify intimately with it"—even though I am certain that our experiences differ.

Black Dialect may be a part of Campbell's intellectual coming of age and mine, but how do we avoid explicitly or implicitly applying these experiences to all other African Americans? What about the African American student who can't identify with any form of Black Dialect? How do we get some of our African American students to remain proud of the ways Black Dialect can be used to construct their personal and cultural identity without deprecating other African Americans who don't bear the same relationship to it?

To summarize, Campbell's study is valuable as far as it goes. However, Campbell missed a golden opportunity to recognize the rhetorical value of dialect (a recognition Campbell admits had not come by the time he completed his project) without ascribing to dialect assumptions about racial ownership.

Valerie Balester's (1993) *Cultural Divide: A Study of African American College-level Writers* similarly pinpoints a particular group of African Americans, four females and four males. Balester is interested not so much in dialect, but rather in the peculiar rhetorical situation in which dialect, as but one vehicle of African American rhetoric, is situated. In other words, whereas Campbell's concern is the rhetorical value of Black English Vernacular itself, Balester's concern is the larger African American rhetorical tradition that makes understanding and appreciating vernacular possible. They both have the same pedagogical objectives: to enable teachers to better serve students who use Black English Vernacular. Hence, Balester carefully surveys the history and use of various forms of African American rhetoric, so that composition teachers, in reading texts written by African American students, would focus on the "rhetorical sophistication" these students already possess. One of the most important dimensions of Balester's study is her observation regarding how these eight college students, to greater or lesser degrees, looked upon the use of Black English Vernacular as improper:

> The BEV speaker is always torn between double voices; the educated SAE brings benefits while it alienates from BEV, and the familiar, homey BEV brings scorn while it establishes solidarity and allows for greater expressiveness. Even those who ridicule SAE speakers and chastise them for "acting white" are aware of this problem and are often willing to concede that "proper" English has value—as long as it is seen as belonging to everyone, not just whites. (15)

Balester compares this sense of doubling to what Du Bois calls "double consciousness," the struggle black people face in reconciling their existence as blacks with the gaze of larger, white society. Balester sees the same type of ambivalence that, for Du Bois, characterized identity and language practices. She is not purposely drawing broad conclusions about the connections among race, dialect, and identity; even so, some of her conclusions point in that direction. While it is true that negative attitudes held by educators toward Black Dialect can certainly be harmful, to pity African American students (such as her student Thomas) for being "unaware that his academically oriented writing bears some hallmarks of African American rhetoric" is extreme. Even if these "hallmarks" do inform Thomas' writing, why couldn't he have the right to construct his authorial identity outside of the Black English Vernacular tradition? At the end of her study, Balester conveys the strong impression that Thomas and Polo, who occasionally "corrects" his friends when they use dialect, are forsaking not a culturally constructed sense of self but an essential self (158).

Balester might be reinforcing the same assumptions regarding the link between dialect and black identity that some of the leaders of the Black Arts Movement embraced. If one is not careful, even the expression "African American Rhetoric" intimates a narrow perception of what constitutes African American identity and experience, not to mention dialect as a component of that rhetoric. Few would deny the significant impact that early black folk and vernacular traditions have had on African Americans, yet the question is: What are the various manifestations of these traditions, and have they influenced all African Americans the same way? How do considerations of gender, class, or sexual orientation generate diverse interpretations of African American Rhetoric? If the term *feminism* should be replaced with the more encompassing *feminisms,* then should not *African American Rhetoric* be replaced with *African American Rhetorics?* The rhetoricity of race itself needs to be exposed.

Neo-Romanticism and Racialized Voice

The collection entitled *Landmark Essays on Voice and Writing,* edited by Peter Elbow, also mirrors the danger of conflating race and voice. Elbow is well known for his neo-Romantic approach to composition studies. His notoriety as an authority on writing is evidenced partly by the popularity of two of his books, *Writing Without Teachers* and *Writing with Power.* I am somewhat skeptical, however, about his use of voice as a metaphor for presence in writing. A pivotal term for Elbow, *voice* is an abstract concept and, as such, is difficult to consistently incorporate into concrete discussions about composition pedagogy. In the *Landmark* collection, he exacerbates that abstract stance by juxtaposing it with an even more abstract stance on racialized voice.

In the introduction to the collection, Elbow sets out to reconcile the binaries surrounding the voice debate. These include discourse as text versus discourse as voice, ethos as real virtue versus ethos as the appearance of virtue, and voice as self versus voice as a role. The first Elbow calls the "overarching debate"; the second, "the traditional debate in rhetoric"; and the third, the "modern debate." In the second part of this introductory essay, Elbow ironically contends that to begin reconciling these opposing positions, certain distinctions must be made:

> The best way to deal with these debates about voice and writing is to distinguish between the *different senses* of voice. We don't have to figure out the winners and losers in these binary and ideological disputes if we apply the terms with more discrimination. In this longer part of my introduction I will first explore some of the features of literal, physical voice as applied to writing: (1) audible voice or intonation (the sounds in a text); (2) dramatic voice (the character or implied author in the text); (3) recognizable or distinctive voice; (4) voice with authority; (5) resonant voice or presence. By making these distinctions, I think I can confine the ideological dispute to the fifth meaning—the only meaning that requires a link between the known text and the unknown actual author. That is, I think I can show that the first four senses of voice in writing are sturdy, useful, and relatively noncontroversial. (1994)

After reading Elbow's introduction, however, these distinctions are not clear. In fact, he merely extends the metaphor of voice to an analogy of the entire body, while managing to maintain the same sense of elusiveness and abstractness that imbued his earlier attempts to define voice in writing. For my purposes, a more profound error is the way Elbow's introduction and the collection itself collapses "audible voice" and "voice with authority" into "resonant voice" or presence. As I have already alluded to, the interchange among these three delineations of voice has particular import for the construction of black voice. Thus, one of Elbow's justifications for resonant voice—namely that "it points to the relationship between discourse and unconscious"—is troubling. Even if such a relationship exists, one could not teach it. Nevertheless, Elbow goes on to complicate voice by including in this collection two essays by African Americans. Both essayists connect Black Dialect to their respective learning experiences. However, the first, by bell hooks, is personal; the other, by June Jordan, is more overtly pedagogical. hooks' essay centers around her experience as the only black student in an all-white creative writing class at Stanford:

> When I became a student in college creative writing classes, I learned a notion of "voice" as embodying the distinctive expression of an individual writer. Our efforts to become poets were to be realized in this coming into awareness and expression of one's voice. In all my writing classes, I was the only black student. Whenever I read a poem written in a particular dialect of Southern black speech, the teacher and the fellow students would praise me for using my "true," authentic voice, and encouraged me to develop this "voice," to write more of these poems. From the onset this troubled me. Such comments seemed to mask racial biases about what my *authentic voice would or should be.* (1994, 52, emphasis mine)

In reality, according to hooks, it was in the segregated schools of the South that she and her peers learned that "our sense of self, and by definition our voice, was not unilateral, monologist, or static, but rather multidimensional." Thus, they "were as at home in dialect as . . . in standard English." hooks alludes to two crucial matters about voice that Elbow either ignores or misunderstands: (1) so-called written voice (as some composition scholars employ that expression) can be understood as a sociolinguistic construction; and (2) dialects, Black or Standard American (and race itself, I argue), can be used to construct identity.

Jordan's essay focuses on the role of Black Dialect in the public sphere, what I called "the marketplace" previously in this article. The essay recalls a course Jordan taught, "In Search of the Invisible Black Woman." What began as a survey of African American women writers of the nineteenth and twentieth centuries ended up as an analysis of the politics of language, fueled by unexpected negative responses on the part of Jordan's black students to the dialect depicted in Alice Walker's *The Color Purple.*

Surprised by this reaction, Jordan led her students to translate an excerpt of Walker's dialect into Standard American English. The results were telling:

> Our process of translation exploded with hilarity and even hysterical, shocked laughter. The Black writer, Alice Walker, knew what she was doing! If the rudimentary criteria for good fiction includes the manipulation of language so that

> the syntax and diction of sentences will tell you the identity of the speakers,
> the probable age and sex and class of the speakers, and even the locale—
> urban/rural/southern/western—then Walker had written, perfectly. (1994, 61)

Jordan underscores the complexity of depicting the nuances of Black English via print. Following the translation exercise with the Walker passage, Jordan remarks:

> Most of the students had never before seen a written facsimile of the way they
> talk. None of the students had ever learned how to read and write their own
> verbal system of communication: Black English. Alternatively, this fact began
> to baffle or else bemuse and then infuriate my students. Why not? Was it too
> late? Could they learn how to do it, now? And, ultimately, the final test ques-
> tion, the one testing my sincerity: Could I teach them? Because I had never
> taught anyone Black English and, as far as I knew, no one, anywhere in the
> United States, had ever offered such a course, the best I could say was "I'll
> try." (62)

The tone of this passage is just as revealing as the content. For Jordan, her students learning to read and write Black English involves more than broadening their repertoire of rhetorical strategies; it represents the effort to claim intellectual property, something that belongs to them in more than a sociolinguistic or cultural sense: it is racially and, therefore, existentially theirs. I am not quite sure how this differs, if at all, from the triad of race, language, and identity, reified during the Black Arts Movement.

If we are to rid ourselves of racialized baggage and move from black writing to writing black, the rhetoricity of race must stressed. If one of the elements of an alternative paradigm of racialized voice is this openness to continual shifting among and reformulating of racial designations, then how do you create moments of community? This question is also relevant given the views about semantic indeterminacy and cultural pluralism that characterize postmodernism.

The question is partly addressed by creating tentative moments of community to which you afford tentative regard. This community is needed for a number of reasons, including to create solidarity and to isolate an agreed-upon strategy for communicating. The slave narrative illustrates the sociopolitical value of constructing collective racial identity. Because the assumption of inhumanity was imposed on Africans since at least the sixteenth century, their first literate responses during the late-eighteenth and nineteenth centuries had to offer unified definitions of group identity in order to form a unified effort to dismantle America's racist paradigm. Blacks as a group, then, have defended their humanity, and they must continue to do so. Race as a way of writing affords the best historical, ideological, and pedagogical response to the dilemma that this essay poses: How do you destabilize narrow definitions of race, even those posited by African Americans, without devaluing African American culture?

Race and voice are important because they can be used to map territory, create community, and ensure an ongoing sense of self- and group-affirmation. But the operative term must remain *uses,* or *serve,* if you will. For race and voice must serve us rhetorically.

Notes

1. According to Henry Louis Gates, Jr., one of the adverse effects of the Black Arts Movement was the inversion of white-race essentialism. Instead of "blackness" symbolizing the essence of nothingness, vice, and stupidity, the leaders of this movement argued that "blackness" actually signified the essence of substance, virtue, and ultimate knowledge. Ironically, this move opened the space for reductive ways of delineating black identity among African Americans. (See *The Signifying Monkey,* Chapter Six.)

2. In *The Signifying Monkey,* Gates explains Reed's major strategies for critiquing the Western tradition, the Harlem Renaissance, and the Black Arts Movement. The title *Mumbo Jumbo* refers both to whites' disdain for black culture and a Swahili term (*jambo* and its plural, *mambo*), which means "What's happening?" And in countering the Euro-American notion of "blackness as negative essence, as a natural transcendent, signified," Reed implicitly offers "a critique of blackness as a presence, which is merely another transcendent signified," a belief embraced during the Black Arts Movement. The reader is encouraged to refer to Gates' superb analysis of *Mumbo Jumbo* in *The Signifying Monkey,* Chapter Six.

Works Cited

Balester, Valerie M. 1993. *Cultural Divide: A Study of African-American College-Level Writers.* Portsmouth, NH: Boynton/Cook.

Campbell, Kermit Ernest. 1993. *The Rhetoric of Black English Vernacular: A Study of the Oral and Written Practices of African American Male College Students.* Dissertation. The Ohio State University.

Christian, Barbara. 1994. "The Race for Theory." *Within the Circle: An Anthology of African American Literary Criticism from the Harlem Renaissance to the Present.* Ed. Angelyn Mitchell. Durham, NC: Duke University Press, 348–359.

Corbett, Edward (ed.). 1974. "The Students' Right to Their Own Language." *College Composition and Communication.* 40: 1–32.

Elbow, Peter (ed.). 1994. *Landmark Essays on Voice and Writing.* Davis, CA: Hermagoras Press.

———. 1981. *Writing With Power.* New York: Oxford University Press.

———. 1973. *Writing Without Teachers.* New York: Oxford University Press.

Gates, Henry Louis, Jr. 1992. *Loose Canons: Notes on the Culture Wars.* New York: Oxford University Press.

———. 1988. *The Signifying Monkey: A Theory of African American Literature.* New York: Oxford University Press.

Gilyard, Keith. 1991. *Voices of the Self: A Study of Language Competence.* Detroit: Wayne State University Press.

Heath, Shirley Brice. 1983. *Ways with Words: Language, Life, and Work in Communities and Classrooms.* New York: Cambridge University Press.

hooks, bell. 1994. "'When I Was a Young Soldier for the Revolution': Coming to Voice." *Landmark Essays on Voice and Writing.* Ed. Peter Elbow. Davis, CA: Hermagoras Press. 51–58.

Jordan, June. 1994. "Nobody Mean (sic) More to Me Than You and the Future Life of Willie Jordan." *Landmark Essays on Voice and Writing.* Ed. Peter Elbow. Davis, CA: Hermagoras Press. 59–72.

Jordan, Winthrop D. 1977. *White Over Black: American Attitudes Toward the Negro, 1550–1812.* New York: Norton.

LaBov, William. 1970. *The Study of Nonstandard English.* Urbana, IL: National Council of Teachers of English.

Neal, Larry. 1994. "The Black Arts Movement." *Within the Circle: An Anthology of African American Literary Criticism from the Harlem Renaissance to the Present.* Ed. Angelyn Mitchell. Durham, NC: Duke University Press, 184–198.

Reed, Ishmael. 1972. *Mumbo Jumbo.* New York: Macmillan.

Smitherman, Geneva. 1977. *Talkin and Testifyin: The Language of Black America.* Boston: Houghton Mifflin.

Woolfe, George C. 1985. *The Colored Museum.* New York: Grove Weidenfeld.

Wright, Richard. 1994. "Blueprint for Negro Writing." *Within the Circle: An Anthology of African American Literary Criticism from the Harlem Renaissance to the Present.* Ed. Angelyn Mitchell. Durham, NC: Duke University Press. 97–106.

6

Racing (Erasing) White Privilege in Teacher/Research Writing About Race

Amy Goodburn

To put our beliefs on hold is to cease to exist as ourselves for a moment—and that is not easy. It is painful as well, because it means turning yourself inside out, giving up your own sense of who you are, and being willing to see yourself in the unflattering light of another's angry gaze. It is not easy, but it is the only way to learn what it might feel like to be someone else and the only way to start a dialogue.

Lisa Delpit
Other People's Children:
Cultural Conflict in the
Classroom

Perhaps one of the most difficult beliefs to interrogate, to examine from another's angry gaze, is the construct of race. The recent heightened dialogue about race construction in the United States—examinations of how people are defined by racial categories and questions about how these descriptions are constructed in relation to an often invisible white norm—has been unsettling for many. Even before the O. J. Simpson trial divided the opinions of Americans along so-called racial lines, the covers of *Time* and *Newsweek* were proclaiming headlines such as "Planet of the White Guys" and "Growing Up Black and White," respectively. In addition to *Ms.* magazine's increasing focus on the needs of women of color, fashion magazines like *Elle* and *Glamour* have begun to include articles about race, such as Naomi Wolf's "The Racism of Well-meaning White People." On talk shows, news programs, and college campuses, race is a topic of dialogue everywhere.

Of course, this attention to race is certainly not new to English Studies, where pedagogical and curricular issues have long been theorized with respect to issues of race, class, and gender. Within literary studies, it has become commonplace to argue for including texts that have been traditionally excluded from the academy because they are not written by white male authors. Within composition studies, researchers are increasingly becoming aware of the ways that the discourses and literacy practices of students of color have been devalued in school settings. Moreover, educators who advocate critical and multicultural pedagogies long have been examining the ways that students' experiences in schools are shaped by social constructs of difference. For the most part, all of these groups usually conclude with calls for "differences" to be valued as resources rather than deficits in the classroom. In these ways, educators argue, students (and texts) who are defined as "other" will be given a space within English Studies.

But in focusing so much on social constructs of difference in terms of the "other," English teachers (most of whom are white) have not fully considered the implications of theorizing their own racial positions in terms of their "whiteness."[1] Thus far, there has been little questioning of how white teachers relate these discussions about difference with respect to their own positions of power and privilege, nor has there been much examination of how these discourses connect to—or are absent from—their teaching and research practices within writing classrooms. The implications for this absence of discussion about race with respect to white teachers' positions are far-reaching. As Beverly Moss and Keith Walters argue in "Rethinking Diversity: Axes of Difference in the Writing Classroom," issues of diversity "challenge us to give great thought to who we are, why we use language and literacy as we do in our professional and private lives, and what roles language and literacy play in the construction of our identity, as well as the identities of those we believe to be similar to and different from us—inside and outside the classroom" (1993, 135). How we construct the identities of others in terms of race and acknowledge (or fail to acknowledge) the privileges and power attendant upon our own raced positions in the classroom raises ethical questions about the ways that we construct our research agendas, carry out these projects in our classrooms, and disseminate the results of these projects to others.

In this essay, I examine several spheres of "race construction" and the ethical implications of these constructions for how I—as a white composition teacher/researcher—named, described, and interpreted student response in a dissertation chapter I wrote on a student discussion of Toni Morrison's *The Bluest Eye* within a writing course focused on "difference." This essay describes my own process of coming to understand the ways that my readings of classroom events were/are shaped by my position as a white teacher/researcher and the implications for understanding what naming these moments might mean for others engaged in composition research. In particular, I examine three different contexts in which my racial position informed (or remained invisible in) my analysis of these classroom scenes. First, I describe how I collected data on the initial class discussion of *The Bluest Eye* and why I selected this class-room moment as significant within the context of my research about multicultural writing classrooms. Second, I examine the taxonomy that I used to situate several different students' written and oral responses to this discussion and the ways that this construct diverted attention from the importance of race, as well as veiled my own position as a white interpreter of these responses. And third, I examine the implications for the ways that this research was disseminated and received within the composition community as I engaged in my job search.

Rereading the various spheres of race construction embedded within these scenes highlights the complexities inherent in studying and writing about how students respond to issues of difference, like race, within writing classrooms. By reflecting on some of the difficulties, however, I hope to raise consciousness about the privilege of white researchers within composition studies' accounts of writing classrooms, as well as to begin to suggest how this awareness might change how we discuss and write about issues of difference in ways that do not appropriate or co-opt "others." Ultimately, then, this essay aims to suggest strategic interventions for how constructs of race can be described and theorized within composition studies research.

Racing the Subject in Composition Studies

The issue of race with respect to the teaching and researching of writing class-rooms has not been totally absent in composition studies. Theorists and scholars interested in anti-racist and critical pedagogies have focused for years on the ways that students resist notions of white privilege. For instance, critical educators like Cy Knoblauch and Jody Swilky have examined how teachers might disrupt or intervene in the hegemonic notions of white privilege that students bring to their reading and writing about texts. And not surprisingly, English teachers of color have long investigated how their racial locations are read by students within their classrooms. For instance, doris davenport's "Dismantling White/Male Supremacy" chronicles her experiences as a "black-feminist-lesbian-working-class-Southern poet" teaching a class with "two black wimmin and twenty-two 'invisible ethnics' (whitefolks)" (1992, 59, 61). In "Racism and the Marvelous Real," Cecilia Rodriguez Milanes describes her experiences as a "Latina instructor of alternative pedagogy" who taught a majority of Long Islanders, a minority of white working-class students, and a handful from "racially diverse, depressed, and violent areas of New York City" (246). And in "The Teacher as Racial/Gendered Subject," Cheryl Johnson describes her experiences as a black woman who teaches the literature of black women writers to primarily white students from middle-class backgrounds.

These teachers speak to the difficulties inherent in raising issues like white privilege in the classroom, foregrounding their own bodies as the embodiment of the racial "other" and emphasizing the ways that students might challenge and educate each other. As Adriana Hernandez notes, the population of the classroom is one of the most valuable resources for analyzing and critiquing constructions of difference. In summarizing different feminist teachers' experiences in the classroom, Hernandez writes:

> The presence of other people in the classroom articulating resistance to the norm provides the possibility to work in a dialogical process. In this way, different voices can be heard, the material is not presented in linear mode as "fact," and knowledge gets produced as a process. (1994, 320)

However, even in discussions about the need for multicultural pedagogies, few white teachers and researchers have begun to consider the implications of their own racial positions for how they read, interpret, and write about their students. In fact, as Christine Sleeter discusses in "How White Teachers Construct Race," the predominantly white teaching force within the United States is rarely asked to examine its own racial identity. In her study of teachers participating in a year-long multicultural workshop, Sleeter observed two common responses that white teachers held toward racial identity — of themselves and of their students — in their classrooms. The first response was that white teachers tended to deny the salience of race as a factor in their classrooms by arguing that they are "color-blind" in their teaching. Because they viewed themselves as "not seeing" racial differences in their students, they argued that they treated all students the same. The second response involved teachers who did acknowledge race as an important factor in students' lives, but emphasized cultural notions of "assimilation" as a means of giving students of color access to social institutions. In other words, white teachers wanted to provide ways for these students to assimilate within white culture without questioning the nature of these social institutions, particularly as they are tied to white privilege. Sleeter found that these white teachers (whom she names Euro-Americans) view participation in ethnic identity as an individual choice, associated with one's private family history rather than a collective experience shaped by social structures. Drawing on Peter McLaren's term *raceless subjectivity,* Sleeter suggests that for these teachers, being white is a position that seemingly transcends race.

In the same vein, Sharon Stockton's *College English* essay, "Blacks vs. Browns," describes how her students' responses to texts emphasized the ways that the "authenticity" of the white man or woman is presented as "transcending" race, collapsing constructs of whiteness into universal characteristics that are raceless. Stockton argues that such binary logic about race allows white teachers to be silent observers, detached and uncritiqued in relation to positions of race in ways that reify their own positions while denying the realities of their students' lives. The consequences of white teachers not examining their notions of "raceless subjectivity" are far-reaching, particularly with respect to how they view (and judge) the experiences of students of color in relation to such an invisible white norm. With the exception of the Webster Groves Action Research Project, whose teacher-researchers shifted their initial questions of how to improve the writing of black students to how to raise consciousness of white teachers about multiple forms of literacy (Krater, Zeni, and Devlin Cason 1994), there are few narratives of white teachers describing and interrogating their own positions as raced subjects within writing classrooms.

Given this absence of consciousness by white teachers about their raced positions in classrooms, it's not surprising that much composition research within writing classrooms also avoids discussions of how white researchers' interpretations of classroom moments are raced. Thus far, there has been little interrogation of what it means to be a white researcher with respect to ethnographic authority in writing research. As Gesa Kirsch and Joy Ritchie note, most researchers do little more than include a statement or "confession" of positions ("as a white, female, middle-class researcher") in order to respond to the critique that one's position is always partial and situated (1995, 9). But, as Peter McLaren suggests, such confessions fail to analyze forms of white ethnicity, thus making white culture "able to occupy the position of the privileging signifier and position in a fixed relation of binary opposition to people of color" (1993, 224). Of course, it's easy to understand teachers' notions of "raceless subjectivity," given the ways that larger cultural discourses about race operate in the United States. As Russell Ferguson suggests:

> In our society, dominant discourse tries never to speak its own name. Its authority is based on absence. The absence is not just that of the various groups classified as "other," although members of these groups are routinely denied power. It is also the lack of any overt acknowledgment of the specificity of the dominant culture, which is simply assumed to be the all-encompassing norm. This is the basis of its power. (1990, 11)

It is this power to remain silent, to view oneself as a "raceless subjectivity" in relation to others who are raced, that allows white teachers and researchers not to question how their own actions in the classroom are shaped by their raced positions. Consequently, many are now calling for white teachers and researchers not only to acknowledge their own investments and privileges with respect to race, but also to interrogate and reread their actions in light of these investments. For instance, in her essay "White Is a Color!," Leslie Roman argues that it is important to recognize whiteness as a structural power relation, an institutionalized whiteness that, both individually and collectively, confers cultural, political, and economic power. In recognizing the ways that whiteness shapes white researchers' readings, Roman, like Kirsch and Ritchie, describes her goal as "critical socially contested realism," a process that goes beyond merely confessing disclaimers of privilege and "aims to treat as its legitimate texts for collective deconstruction all claims to know and represent reality made in the classroom, including those of the teacher, those manifest in the formal and hidden curriculum, and those implicit in classroom social relations" (1991, 83). Similarly, Peggy McIntosh's "White Privilege: Unpacking the Invisible Knapsack" examines more concretely the daily effects of white privilege by laying out twenty-six conditions or assumptions that were "passed on" to her as a white person (1990, 32).

One way to begin deconstructing "these claims to know" is by making visible white people's participation within these texts. For instance, theorist Ruth Frankenberg has begun to name and describe the racialness of white experience with the phrase *the Social Construction of Whiteness,* a standpoint and a set of discursive practices from which white people look at themselves, others, and society. As Frankenburg (1993) suggests, to use the term *whiteness* is to assign everyone a place in the relations of racism because it "asserts that there are locations, discourses, and material relations to which the term *whiteness* applies—these locations are intrinsically linked to unfolding relations of dominance" (6). Based on her study of life-history interviews with thirty white women, Frankenberg attempts to describe the "discursive repertoires" or strategies for thinking through race that are learned, drawn upon, and enacted through cultural practices in people's lives. In keeping with poststructuralist views of the subject that view material experience and discursive dimensions as integrally interconnected, Frankenburg aims to examine how discursive repertoires of race, particularly "whiteness," generate and continually transform the ways that people think about and act upon their own raced assumptions (22).

Of course, naming and interrogating what constitutes "whiteness" is not without its problems. As AnnLouise Keating's (1995) essay "Interrogating 'Whiteness,' (De)Constructing 'Race'" cautions, theorists interested in naming constructs of "whiteness" oftentimes reinforce fixed categories of racialized meanings that perpetuate and support negative stereotypes. Keating's misgivings about emphasizing "whiteness" or other racialized identities within classroom pedagogies stem from her experiences with class discussions in which self-identified white students were made to feel guilty about their privileged positions (915). Like Keating, I am dubious of the extent to which pedagogies that ask students to name "whiteness" in literary texts enables them to resist existing stereotypes. While I support pedagogies that seek to empower students through studying and understanding the role that "difference" plays in people's lives, I think that the lens needs to be shifted away from reading our students' responses to texts and onto how we, as teachers and researchers, read and write our students as "raced" texts.

Toward this end, this essay examines the discursive repertoires that I used for thinking about race when I was researching and writing about multicultural pedagogies within my dissertation research. Like Frankenburg, I believe that the discursive repertoires we use for thinking about race in our research are integrally connected to the material conditions of our classrooms. In reflecting on the research text that I produced in a study of multicultural writing classrooms, then, I am interested in critically rereading the discursive repertoires I used to write about these classroom scenes. How did my research process—the selection and analysis of data, the "writing up" of interpretations, and the dissemination of results—contradict, conceal, and/or explain away (in Frankenburg's terms) the materiality of the classroom and the larger social context in ways that reveal my complicity and perhaps investment in racist structures and attitudes? And what are the implications for how I read these cultural narratives of race, in terms of my own classroom and in terms of contributing to research accounts in composition studies?

In the winter of 1993, I conducted an ethnographic study of three college-level writing classrooms focused on issues of difference.[2] Because I was interested in theories of critical pedagogy and social-oriented pedagogies within composition studies, I intended to examine how teachers and students negotiated writing and talking about difference in writing classes centered around these issues. In the chapter I discuss, I was a participant-observer in a class of eighteen students: ten men (eight white, one African American, and one African American/Native American); eight women (six white and two African American); and a white woman teacher. As a participant-observer, I sat with the students each class period, taking field notes, audiotaping discussions, and participating in small groups and class activities. I also periodically interviewed the teacher and the students throughout the term. This class was a second-level writing course focused on issues of difference within the United States through the study of literature.

As a graduate student who was interested in social-oriented pedagogies within education in general and composition studies in particular, I was familiar with the literature about social constructs of "difference." From the onset, then, I assumed that I knew what "difference" was. After all, I had read the work of critical educators such as Michael Apple, Henry Giroux, Shirley Grundy, bell hooks, and Patti Lather, as well as radical compositionists such as Mark Hurlbert, Susan Jarratt, and Ira Shor. I had studied theories of resistance and hegemony, of multiple subjectivities and positionalities, and I was committed to pedagogies that raised student consciousness about how their own experiences are shaped by these social discourses. What this literature did not prepare me for was the way that my lens as a white woman researcher shaped the ways that I was interpreting student and teacher behavior through the terministic screen of race.

White-ing Out Researcher Authority

The first sphere of race construction that I'd like to examine centers around a single classroom discussion on Toni Morrison's *The Bluest Eye* and the decisions I made in selecting, reconstructing, and analyzing this classroom moment. Rereading the choices I made in representing this discussion illuminates how my ethnographic authority as a researcher was "whited out" or seemingly assumed to be a "raceless subjectivity" within the chapter entitled "Students Negotiating Textual Authority" that I produced. From the onset, the decisions I made about what was "significant" about this discussion and how to describe this significance were shaped by my position as a white researcher and the frameworks that I relied on to theorize this position. To illustrate the nature of my assumptions, I present three paragraphs from this chapter that describe how students discussed *The Bluest Eye* and why this discussion was significant for understanding the students' responses with respect to difference:

> The discussion began with Ann [the teacher] asking students to write questions that they had about the book. After collecting these questions, Ann asked students to describe their overall responses in reading. Some students called it "vile" and "obscene." One said that it was "rude" and "graphic" while another said it was "realistic" and "true to life." Some said the ending was too abrupt and left the reader hanging. Others said it was too depressing, and one student said that the novel was written only "to get a rise out of you, to shock you." This statement led Ann [the teacher] to ask, "Is there anything else in this book besides pure shock value? What else did you guys get out of it?" The students' responses reflected how they viewed the purpose of the texts in general. Several students commented on literary aspects, saying it has "a lot of symbolism," or "the writing is very descriptive" while others described it in more prescriptive terms as "an educational tool" and "a good moral."
>
> The discussion of *TBE*'s value as a text soon moved into a discussion of themes that students found significant. For the first forty minutes students comfortably discussed issues of difference on a wide range of topics, including gender and sexual politics in the characters' lives, the portrayal of religion and hypocrisy, and the book's explicit language. In the last twenty minutes, however, the discussion turned to the issue of race. Some argued that the novel is a commentary on how standards of beauty are tied to race, with white culture setting standards that devalue other cultures. A few interpreted the novel as a condemnation of interracial conflict within black communities, while still others argued that the novel illuminates the struggles of those who are trying to achieve the American dream. The students quickly became polarized around the question: "Is racism a focus of this text?" Some students argued that racism is an important issue in the novel while others argued that readers would have to be "looking for" racism in order to see it as significant. The discussion soon came to an impasse and one woman, visibly upset by the students' comments, asked Ann to end it. Ann agreed, gave the students a short break, and when the students returned she directed them to a peer response session.
>
> I have chosen to focus in detail on *The Bluest Eye* discussion and the students' and teacher's subsequent responses to it because this classroom moment was representative of how students engaged in talking and writing about issues of difference throughout the term in relation to Ann's pedagogical goals. Besides my own fascination with how the discussion became polarized as

soon as racial difference became an issue, students also were interested in accounting for the classroom tensions and misunderstandings that this discussion seemed to produce. Although *TBE* discussion was never resumed as a
class, almost all of the students continued to write about it in their response
papers, with most of them referring to the discussion explicitly (many even
noted the date). When I interviewed students about the course, most of them
still wanted to talk about this particular discussion. Ann's reading of this class
discussion was further reflected in a response she wrote to one of the students.
Thus, this class discussion seemed an especially fruitful site for exploring how
and why students responded to Ann's pedagogical goals in foregrounding issues of difference in the texts that they read. (Goodburn 1994, 84–86)

The first issue I want to examine from this excerpt is the way that I chose
to write about this class discussion and the position I adopted in "writing it up"
as I did, particularly in terms of either including or not including racial identities in my written analysis. At the time that I originally wrote about this discussion, I felt competing tensions and conflicts in how to represent it. While I
felt that it was an important moment in the classroom—particularly as it related to my research focus on how students and teachers negotiate authority in
multicultural writing classrooms—I also knew that it was impossible to extract
its significance from the context of the discussions that preceded and followed
it. Moreover, I was highly conscious of the ethics involved in representing this
scene. I had read Kenneth Burke and knew that whatever terministic screen I
selected would necessarily involve a deflection of other interpretations. I knew
that I could not possibly be "objective," and yet I wanted this classroom moment to have some ethnographic authority, to legitimize why I recorded this
scene instead of others, for instance, and to argue for its relevance in terms of
the overall focus of this chapter, as well as the entire dissertation.

In considering how much context to provide in the first paragraph, for instance, I chose not to use identity markers such as gender or race to describe
the students who made these comments. Because I was using these few paragraphs as a springboard for discussing the different positions that I saw students adopting throughout the class in their written and oral responses, I did not
want to "tip my hand" by elaborating on these contributors' social positions.
For instance, the second to last sentence in the second paragraph would have
read much differently if I had written, "one white woman, visibly upset by the
comments of an African American woman, asked Ann [the teacher] to end it."
The text also would have read much differently if I had described the polariza-
tion of the discussion as being between white and black students. In trying to
render an "objective" representation of what was said without identifying the
participants in terms of their social identities, I stripped much of the context
from this description.

Indeed, what I don't say in the original text is that I found it exceedingly
difficult to write. As a writer, I felt almost paralyzed by describing students
in terms of social categories of difference, in part because so much of my

dissertation was focused on questioning how these categories are used, how students and teachers view them with respect to pedagogy, and the problematics involved in such representation. I was highly conscious of the ways that my own descriptions or labels for students' social positions might reify or perpetuate some of the issues that the chapter itself was intended to problematize. For instance, while I was interested in examining how students position themselves in class discussions in terms of social constructs like race and gender, I also felt it was important to represent the students' own views of themselves with respect to these constructs rather than imposing my own categories. If students didn't define themselves as being raced, for instance, then should I have used terms such as "Euro-American," "Anglo-American," "Caucasian," or "white" to describe them? Who held the power in defining such social identity positions and what are the implications of these definitions for how I read (or misread) their responses? And if I did choose to use social descriptors like these, how much additional context did I need to provide the reader to fairly represent the significance of these positions?

While I knew quite a lot about the students' backgrounds and histories after being a participant observer in this class for ten weeks, I had no clear idea of which details to include to fairly render and account for the complexity of their responses. For instance, if I used only race or gender descriptors, then readers still wouldn't be able to appreciate how the nineteen-year-old African American woman's reading of *The Bluest Eye* was shaped by her experiences in a women's studies class, her despondency over the recent death of her mother's fiancé, and her newfound commitment to political activism. These were the issues that I struggled with at the time I was writing this chapter and, although most of the literature I read about ethnography argued the need to provide context, little of it discussed the problematics of representation in these terms.

But beyond the struggles that I can recall when writing this text, these three paragraphs also reflect more unconscious assumptions I held in writing about this discussion, assumptions that "whited out" my presence in the text and that call for further examination of the authority I assumed in writing about this classroom scene. First, my decision not to name the participants in this discussion allowed me to veil my own participation under the guise of the "objective" ethnographic recorder. That is, I do not describe what I was doing during this discussion or say whether I was a contributor to it. Nor does this description include my responses to or interpretations of the discussion. Although I wrote a research journal about the discussion that night, that information is not incorporated in these paragraphs.

Despite these attempts to render an "objective" recording of the discussion by consciously erasing myself from the text, however, my assumptions as a white woman "recording" this scene are still revealed. For instance, my ethnographic authority is illuminated in the second paragraph when I describe how "For the first forty minutes, students comfortably discussed issues of difference on a wide range of topics . . ." and "students quickly became polarized as soon as racial difference became an issue." Not only do I describe what students said in this discussion, I also interpret the discussion as being relatively "comfortable" for them. In the same way that my decision not to include racial identity tags veiled the ways that students' racial positions shaped the dynamics of this discussion, my language in this paragraph reifies my invisible authority as a white researcher to interpret the dynamics. In other words, what did I mean by the term *comfortable* and why did I apply it to this classroom setting? As a teacher, I do not subscribe to the view that classrooms are "safe spaces" for students, and Ann's stated goals as a teacher were to disrupt and challenge students' notions with an oppositional and conflict-driven pedagogy. So why did I use this language in my field notes to describe this scene? How was I interpreting this comfort level and for whom? The teacher? The white students? The African American students? Or for me? Why did I view this discussion in terms of the participants' comfort levels to begin with, and what are the implications for the ways that I read it as polarized as soon as the issue of race began to be raised?

In rereading the assumptions laden in my original text, I am not arguing that the "turn" in this discussion was entirely a figment of my imagination or solely a projection of my own fears as a white woman uncomfortable with hostile arguments about race in the classroom. As the third paragraph of my original text suggests, the students' own preoccupation with this discussion was manifested in their response journals, interviews, and subsequent class discussions. But in reflecting on the ways that I constructed this text, I find it interesting that I didn't problematize these paragraphs in a way that revealed my own investments and assumptions inherent in focusing on this discussion to begin with. For example, in describing "my own fascination with how the discussion became polarized as soon as racial difference became an issue," I did not feel compelled to justify *why* I found it fascinating or how this fascination was perhaps tied to my own position as a white woman researcher invested in examining issues of difference. Indeed, in giving only one sentence to my own interest, this paragraph seems to try to justify why I felt the discussion was important more in terms of student and teacher interest, rather than in terms of my own investments.

Beyond these three paragraphs and even the entire forty-three–page chapter, it's also important to question why I focused on issues of race only in the classroom populated with students of color. In the other two chapters devoted to analysis of particular classrooms, I focused on issues of religious authority and gender. While at the time these issues seemed to be the most important factors shaping student response (in one class, seven of the students identified themselves as Fundamentalist Christians, a fact that certainly shaped that particular class' dynamics), when considered within the larger context of my research project about issues of difference, this absence of discussion about race in the all-white classrooms is troubling. Why did I not examine how the all-white population of students in the other two classes that I observed located their authority to read and write about texts in terms of the social construct of race?

McLaren's notion of "raceless subjectivity" is connected, I think, to the ways that I allowed my own position of whiteness to remain uninterrogated in my gaze of these three classrooms. Although all three classes read texts about race and racism and had lively discussions about racism in U.S. culture, I did not find the classroom scenes within the all-white classrooms to be as interesting or compelling, perhaps because my own assumptions and privileges of whiteness went unchallenged. Because I considered myself a liberal who was acutely aware of how racism is structurally organized within institutions, I did not fully interrogate the white students' responses—which tended to view racism in individual and psychological terms—or my own presumptions in not writing about them. And because the white students generally did not view themselves as even having a race, there was definitely a lesser degree of tension in discussing race issues, a condition that remained unproblematized by them and me throughout the term.

Deferring Race Through Taxonomy

The second sphere of race construction that I wish to examine concerns the taxonomy that I used to structure the students' responses following these initial introductory paragraphs and the ways that this heuristic also deferred and erased issues of race. As suggested previously, when I was writing this chapter, I was fascinated by the ways that students responded to *The Bluest Eye*. In compiling this data, I had primarily a collection of stories—of the classroom discussion, the students' response papers, and the interviews in which students retold the story of the discussion through their own perspectives. But I didn't have a framework for making sense of these stories. When I first started writing about them, I had pages and pages of narrative that included excerpts from all of these different contexts to account for how and why students responded in the ways that they did. This draft did render the complexity of these multiple perspectives. It also was unreadable. Members of my dissertation committee suggested that I create a taxonomy to help "order" these students' responses in some way. As they continually told me, I needed to make an argument about the data, one that could contribute to conversations already ongoing within composition studies and the discourses of critical pedagogy. In essence, I was faced with the rhetorical dilemma that most researchers face: claiming authority and validity for one's interpretations in the "writing up" of the data, as well as positioning one's interpretations within the discourse community that one wishes to enter.

After reviewing the data that I so highly valued but couldn't explain the significance of to others, I decided to use a taxonomy that would help distinguish and compare different students' oral and written responses. Borrowing from Giroux's use of the term *the politics of location,* I chose to categorize by pairs six of the students' responses with regard to their own politics of location, first as a means of defining the varying stances that students took to *The Bluest Eye* in their oral and written responses, and second as a means of exploring the limits of these locations for students' assumptions about how texts can and should be read in general.

For instance, in the first pairing of students, I profiled Pat and Vaughn, a white male and an African American male, respectively, whose assumptions about texts as repositories of authors' meanings shaped the ways that they could respond both to *The Bluest Eye* and to their classmates' responses to it. In supporting the categories of the taxonomy, I provided examples from these students' written response papers, oral contributions to discussions, and out-of-class interviews to highlight how these six students' literacy assumptions shaped their classroom negotiations. I concluded the chapter by examining the implications of these students' differing locations for how the teacher, who named herself as a critical teacher, could enact a pedagogy designed to examine and value issues of difference. By examining these students' varying assumptions about literacy and where authority of meaning lies within reading, I suggested, the teacher could have better understood the ways that her goals were contested and resisted.

Like any interpretive framework, this taxonomy selected moments and deflected others. In many ways, it allowed me to account for some of the context that was stripped away in the original opening paragraphs. In categorizing the responses and experiences of six individual students, I was able to locate some of these originally "nameless" responses within the context of the students' positions of race, gender, age, educational status, and classroom history. At the same time, however, this taxonomy felt limited in ways that I couldn't fully articulate. There were so many issues of difference shaping students' responses that it was difficult for me to account for them all. And the biggest difference of all—the issue of race—seemed to become submerged within the framework of literacy that I was encouraged to construct. It's not that I wasn't able to discuss issues of race within the chapter; rather, the taxonomy seemed to defer or subsume race as a category of analysis under the larger rubric of literacy or textual authority.

In fact, I was encouraged by some colleagues not to make race constructs and their relationship to student response the priority of the chapter because they felt that such an approach wouldn't "fit" easily into composition studies discourse. One friend who read an early version of this chapter said that I needed to eliminate some of the race theory and put in more composition theory to give the chapter more "weight" and "scholarship." And although I intuitively felt that the students' responses to the text, their assumptions about literacy, and issues of difference were integrally connected, I found it difficult to find a space within composition studies discourse for this discussion.

In organizing this chapter, I also was encouraged to think of my audience in terms of the types of jobs for which I would be applying the following year. I was told that I needed to demonstrate that I was conversant in the literature of composition studies and not just trying to "sneak through the back door" with cultural studies. While I thought that race construction was integrally connected to the discourses of composition studies, I began to question its importance in light of others' responses—which is not to say that I entirely omitted discussions of race within the original text. In the conclusion of the original chapter, for instance, I noted how "for many of the white students, discussions about race meant discussing the lives of people of color, with little sense of how their own racial locations are implicated in the construction of otherness" (Goodburn 1994, 121). But this statement is quickly subsumed by the larger focus on textual assumptions rather than assumptions about how constructions of race in U.S. culture shaped students' readings. In effect, the focus on race became deferred within the organizational structure of the taxonomy, a structure that I used to ground my research in ongoing conversations within composition studies. While I knew that I wasn't satisfied at the time with this organizational structure, I realize now that what I considered solely rhetorical constructs of organization were also political choices in how issues of race were constructed and/or erased.

Racing the Market

The third sphere of race construction in my research took place two months after I finished writing this chapter. Immersed in job-search rituals, I was preparing the "job talk" that I planned to deliver during on-campus interviews. To assist me and two other students who were interviewing, members of my dissertation committee and a few other students served as an audience for our practice talks. Writing this talk was difficult for me because of the multiple audiences to whom I would be speaking. I was visiting the English departments of five different state universities—three in the Midwest, one in the South, and one on the West Coast—all of which held very different assumptions about the value of composition as a research field in general and the goals of multicultural pedagogies in particular. Because I did not want to give a different talk at each institution, I was left with the rhetorical problem of disseminating the results of my research in a way that would appeal to the broadest interests of these varying (and sometimes internally divided) audiences.

Because most of the audiences consisted of faculty who teach literature, I chose to focus on the ways that my research participated in the conversations about multicultural pedagogies with regard to how students read and respond to texts. Consequently, I again returned to the chapter on *The Bluest Eye* discussion, pulling out excerpts that spoke to the ways that the oral and written responses of two of the students from the taxonomy were read (and usually discredited) by the teacher and the other students. I argued that teachers who aim to enact multicultural pedagogies need to take into account the rhetorical context of the classroom, and that using "multicultural" texts as a means of valuing difference is more problematic than current discussions of multicultural pedagogies suggest.

After finishing this practice talk, the audience members posed various questions, asking me to extend the implications of my argument and highlighting places where I needed to provide more context. I was feeling pretty confident about delivering this talk for the on-campus visits when one of my committee members—the only African American person on this committee of three—asked the question, "Why did you choose to pair the stories of Vaughn and Staci in this talk? Why did you choose two African American students' stories when they weren't paired together in your chapter?"

My committee member's questions disarmed me. I hadn't thought much about why I chose these particular students, beyond the fact that I found their stories to be the most interesting of the six students that I had profiled, and I hoped that the audiences would find them interesting as well. Although they had not been paired together in my original taxonomy, I was using the data to construct a slightly different argument than the one in the original chapter, which was directed to an audience of composition scholars rather than literature ones. Moreover, I had more data from these two students than any others in the class because they had continued to write about the impact of *The Bluest Eye* discussion long after other students had abandoned it. But even as I mouthed these responses, I was still unsettled by my committee member's question, just as she looked unsatisfied with my answers.

As I thought about her question more that evening, I began to wonder why I found these two students' responses to be the most interesting. Was it because I found them exotic and other to my own experiences? Why did I not find the politically conservative white male's responses—one of which was an oral contribution of, "Shit. I'm so sick of minority shit" when *The Bluest Eye* was selected by the class—as interesting as the ones that I had selected? The more I began to think about the selections that I had made in composing this job talk, the more I began to feel troubled by the implications of my choices. At the time, I framed my committee member's question about issues of representation within the job talk as a rhetorical problem, a question that led me to consider differently the authority that I was claiming for these stories by using this particular taxonomy. If, indeed, the pairing that I had pulled out of the original text was not accurately representing the students' experiences, then how could I revise it to more fairly represent the data in my dissertation? Upon returning from these campus visits, I revised the original chapter by pairing these two students' responses within this taxonomy.

But even after I finished writing and defending my dissertation, my committee member's question continued to echo in my mind. And as I began to read more critical pedagogical discourses that discussed the politics of race and representation, I began to think about how my own choices of race representation were situated within the larger contexts in which I—as a white female graduate student who desired a tenure-track job within an English department—was participating. These reflections led to larger questions that my committee member might have been hinting at, but (perhaps out of kindness) never explicitly stated and that I, as a white person unconscious of my privileges of whiteness, never fully considered: Was my decision to choose the stories of two African American students for this job talk an unconsciously racist one? Beyond the problematic that I might have found these students' responses interesting because they were exotic or different from myself, was I using their stories as a way of proving my own tolerance or white liberalism? Was I just trying to get on the race bandwagon by showing that I could work with and write about students of color and thus prove that I was a good multicultural hire?

Certainly most of the MLA job advertisements called for candidates who were conscious of multicultural issues and could meet the needs of diverse student populations. How was my decision to focus on these two students an effort to tap into the predominantly white liberal intentions of these hiring committees? What were the ethical implications involved in choosing to speak about these two students when, of the fifty-nine students that I studied in these three classrooms, only four were African American? In effect, why did I, a white teacher who was studying the classrooms of two other white teachers consisting of predominantly white students in a university predominantly populated by white students, decide to write about two African American students' oral and written responses to a discussion about a text written by an African American woman in a course designed to address issues of difference? And, just as significantly, why did no one else on my committee find it problematic for me to do so?

The fact that these questions went unasked by me and most of my colleagues during my job search points to my white privilege in uncomfortable and painful ways. Indeed, asking these questions led me to consider my investments and interests in multicultural and critical pedagogies to begin with. While I had always been attracted to the goals of these pedagogies—committed to examining how issues of difference are defined, represented, and interrogated within the classroom—I never considered the question, "What's in it for me?" What were my own investments in researching these issues, particularly my interest in race and identity? And what were the politics involved in representing myself to other English faculty in terms of these goals? Was I simply participating in the type of discursive games that Hazel Carby (1982) critiques in "White Woman Listen": engaging in the textual discourses of multicultural and critical pedagogies as "fictional substitutes" rather than working to establish real social relationships with racially oppressed people, thereby disavowing myself from my complicity in perpetuating racist educational practices? In effect, was this job talk, and the larger dissertation project from which it was drawn, primarily produced and received as textual currency to participate in the multiculturalism economy of the profession? And what are the implications of the fact that this talk was successful in securing me job offers, while the discursive repertoires of whiteness implicit within it remained unquestioned and uninterrogated? And, most significantly to me now, where does this examination of my own complicity within these discursive relations leave me, as one who still remains committed to the goals of multicultural and critical pedagogies, and yet who is suspicious of her own privileges and investments in researching these issues?

Racing Research with Whiteness

My goal for this essay is not to present a seamless narrative of my research process, a before-and-after story of "once I was a racist researcher/teacher, but now I've seen the light." Understanding racist relations of dominance and my privileges of whiteness as a white woman professor within these relations is much messier, an ongoing project in which I must always work to uncover and struggle against the invisible norms of power that my culture affords me. Indeed, even the production of this text needs to be questioned in terms of how it participates in the relations of dominance that I seek to critique. After all, its publication helps to legitimate my place in the academy—serving as the textual currency that I need to accumulate in my drive for tenure—while perhaps preventing others' texts, including those of researchers of color, from being published.

Some might argue that focusing on constructs of whiteness privileges white liberal guilt and diverts attention away from the material problems that people of color face in and beyond the classroom. I am aware of these criticisms, as well as the concerns that discourses of race can be co-opted and normalized within the profession in ways that participate in and perpetuate racist structures. But given the fact that the overwhelming majority of research within composition studies is written by white researchers and that the teaching force in the United States is increasingly white while the student population increasingly is not, I feel it is imperative to acknowledge that constructions of whiteness are inherent in how we teach and do research and that, therefore, systems of white privilege do need to be interrogated with respect to how students and teachers are textually represented. And I hope that this re-presentation of my own research processes raises questions about how composition researchers can extend their consciousness about how to develop a language of difference to discuss and write about issues of race—including whiteness—in ways that do not "other" others.

But where does all this reflection lead us? As one white friend recently asked, "If whiteness is so invisible, then how are we supposed to be conscious of it? Can we only theorize it after the fact?" The best answer that I could offer is, "It's not that hard, and it's not that simple." Race construction itself is constantly in process and ongoing, a shifting terrain always dependent on provisional contexts. While I am certainly more aware of examining issues of race construction within classrooms of all white students, I can never be fully aware of the ways that my position as a white teacher/researcher privileges me not to see discursive fields of reference that might challenge my authority as an interpreter of raced realities. Like Sleeter, I believe that one of the best ways to deconstruct racism within education is to populate the teaching (and I would add researching) force within the United States with educators of color. Yet the burden to problematize one's own assumptions of whiteness shouldn't fall on the "other." White teachers/researchers should not rely on others to unsettle their own positions of privilege and power.

Writing teachers and researchers have long considered themselves to have a unique vantage point for examining how language instruction participates in racist relations of dominance and for theorizing how new languages of difference can be more developed for anti-racist struggles. Yet it's one thing for teachers to ask students to examine stereotypes in the media and write about how difference has shaped their lives, and quite another to ask teachers and researchers to consider the ways that their projects are implicated in perpetuating racist assumptions and institutional structures. We need to move beyond defining texts as multicultural because they are written by those other to ourselves and begin thinking about how all discourses are inherently raced, through social constructions of whiteness as well as social constructs of color. Moreover, composition teachers and researchers need to examine their own investments in multicultural pedagogies and projects, questioning the extent to which their own assumptions run counter to their proposed anti-racist struggles. Beyond examining the discursive repertoires that students use for discussing or resisting discussions about race, then, we need to question the discursive repertoires and assumptions within which we, as composition researchers and teachers, are located when we write about race—and when we don't.

Notes

1. In this essay, I am purposely using the term *white* instead of other terms such as *Caucasian, Euro-American,* and/or *Anglo-American* to focus particularly on the construct of race. While I recognize that the term *white* refers to a color, not an ethnic identity, and that race is a social construct, not a biological fact, I choose to use the term *white* because it brings to the foreground the popular discourses that currently shape our students' notions of race in ways that the language in academic journals does not. Similarly, I use the terms *people of color, teachers of color,* and so on provisionally, recognizing that their use further perpetuates the construction of a binary opposition between white as the normative position and all other racial positions as *other,* a construction that this essay aims to critique.

2. A more detailed account of the goals and methodologies of the entire study can be found in *Critical Composition Pedagogies and the Question of Authority: Scenes from Three College-Level Writing Classrooms* (Goodburn 1994). For another perspective on the particular class I will be discussing here, see "Collaboration, Critical Pedagogy, and Struggles over Difference" (*Journal of Advanced Composition,* Winter 1994, with Beth Ina).

Works Cited

Carby, Hazel. 1982. "White Woman Listen: Black Feminism and the Boundaries of Sisterhood." *The Empire Strikes Back: Race and Racism in '70's Britain.* London: Hutchinson. 212–235.

davenport, doris. 1992. "Dismantling White/Male Supremacy." *Social Issues in the English Classroom.* Eds. Mark Hurlbert and Samuel Trotten. Urbana, IL: National Council of Teachers of English. 59–75.

Delpit, Lisa. 1995. *Other People's Children: Cultural Conflict in the Classroom.* New York: The New Press.

Ferguson, Russell. 1990. *Out There: Marginalization and Contemporary Culture.* Cambridge, MA: MIT Press.

Frankenberg, Ruth. 1993. *White Women, Race Matters: The Social Construction of Whiteness.* Minneapolis: University of Minnesota Press.

Goodburn, Amy M. 1994. *Critical Composition Pedagogies and the Question of Authority: Scenes from Three College-Level Writing Classrooms.* Dissertation. The Ohio State University.

Goodburn, Amy, and Beth Ina. 1994. "Collaboration, Critical Pedogogy, and Struggles over Difference." *JAC: Journal of Advanced Composition.* 14.1: 131–147.

Hernandez, Adriana. 1994. "Feminist Pedagogy: Experience and Difference in a Politics of Transformation." *College Composition and Communication.* 43: 318–321.

hooks, bell. 1994. *Teaching to Transgress: Education as the Practice of Freedom.* New York: Routledge.

Johnson, Cheryl L. 1994. "The Teacher as Racial/Gendered Subject." *College English.* 56: 409–419.

Keating, AnnLouise. 1995. "Interrogating 'Whiteness,' (De)Constructing 'Race.'" *College English.* 57: 901–918.

Kirsch, Gesa E., and Joy S. Ritchie. 1995. "Beyond the Personal: Theorizing a Politics of Location in Composition Research." *College Composition and Communication.* 46: 7–29.

Knoblauch, Cy H. 1991. "Critical Teaching and the Dominant Culture." *Composition and Resistance.* Eds. Mark Hurlbert and Michael Blitz. Portsmouth, NH: Heinemann. 12–21.

Krater, Joan, Jane Zeni, and Nancy Devlin Cason. 1994. *Mirror Images: Teaching Writing in Black and White.* Portsmouth, NH: Boynton/Cook.

McIntosh, Peggy. 1990. "White Privilege: Unpacking the Invisible Knapsack." *Independent School.* Winter 1990: 31–34.

McLaren, Peter. 1993. "Border Disputes: Multicultural Narrative, Identity Formation, and Critical Pedagogy in Postmodern America." *Naming Silenced Lives.* Eds. Daniel McLaughlin and William Tierney. New York: Routledge. 201–235.

Milanes, Cecilia Rodriguez. 1992. "Racism and the Marvelous Real." *Social Issues in the English Classroom.* Eds. Mark Hurlbert and Samuel Trotten. Urbana, IL: National Council of Teachers of English. 246–257.

Moss, Beverly, and Keith Walters. 1993. "Rethinking Diversity: Axes of Difference in the Writing Classroom." *Theory and Practice in the Teaching of Writing: Rethinking the Discipline.* Ed. Lee Odell. Carbondale, IL: Southern Illinois University Press. 132–185.

Roman, Leslie. 1991. "White Is a Color! White Defensiveness, Postmodernism, and Anti-Racist Pedagogy." *Race Identity and Representation in Education.* Eds. Cameron McCarthy and Warren Crichlow. New York: Routledge. 71–88.

Sleeter, Christine E. 1991. "How White Teachers Construct Race." *Race Identity and Representation in Education.* Eds. Cameron McCarthy and Warren Crichlow. New York: Routledge. 157–71.

Stockton, Sharon. 1995. "Blacks vs. Browns." *College English.* 57: 166–81.

Swilky, Jody. 1993. "Resisting Difference: Student Response to Multicultural Texts." *The Writing Instructor.* Fall 1993: 21–33.

Wolf, Naomi. "The Racism of Well-Meaning White People." *Glamour.* 93 (August 1995): 230–231.

7

Power, Conflict, and Contact: Re-constructing Authority in the Classroom

Robert D. Murray, Jr.

According to legend, Pythagoras, the fifth-century Greek philosopher, lectured to his students while sitting behind a screen so that they could only hear him. We do not have enough information as to why he may have done that, but we can make some fairly good guesses. This Pythagorean model, as I will call it, can teach us a great deal about classroom authority. Ostensibly—and deceptively—anti-authoritarian, the act of hiding removes you as the object of your students' gaze, yet your absence increases the intensity of their attention. It is a kind of invisibility that increases awareness of your presence; making yourself invisible constructs an extraordinary visibility.

To complicate this one model of teacher authority, I would like to offer its opposite, from Nella Larsen's 1928 novel *Quicksand.* Helga Crane, the main character, is a teacher at an all-black college in the fictional Southern community of Naxos. Disillusioned with the academy in general, and her school specifically, Helga reflects on her attempt to maintain a commitment to her ideal classroom:

> Yet she had continued to try not only to teach, but to befriend those happy, singing children, whose charm and distinctiveness the school was so surely so ready to destroy. Instinctively, Helga was aware that their smiling submissiveness covered many poignant heartaches and perhaps much secret contempt for their instructors. But she was powerless. In Naxos between teacher and student, between condescending authority and smoldering resentment, the gulf was too great, and too few had tried to cross it. (5)

These two methods, taken together, can serve as poles in the range of a teacher's authority. In one model, a disembodied voice surrounds students with the content of the lecture; its authority is derived from the god-like implications of the concealed, but obeyed, leader—the one whose face must not be seen. At the other end of the spectrum is the teacher-as-friend, a model that seems to break down even as Helga begins to consider it. Yet, we might say, at least she has the inclination to try something. Aware of the "condescending" version of authority that is in place at Naxos—no doubt a rendition of the Pythagorean model—Helga seeks to counteract the students' resentment with her announced awareness of and compassion for their private, aching lives. But it is to no avail: she is powerless and the gulf between teacher and student is too great.

In some ways, this opposition seems like a prototypical staging of the battle between the "banking" or "mechanist" methodology and the "problem-posing" approach. And Helga's inability to resolve this problem does not exactly chart a course of optimism for those who believe in a liberatory, critical-thinking pedagogy. But to compare the adjustments each teacher has to make in order to create a more thriving learning environment, Helga has less work to do. Her problems are more easily remedied. Her difficulties are caused by attempting to establish an emotional and not a political relationship with her students. A better course of action would have been to recognize her own disempowerment and then use it as a way to bridge the gulf she perceives between her and her students. However, this brings about its own set of questions. Does Helga, thus identified as powerless, become a spokesperson for disempowerment? If so, can she speak authoritatively about canonical texts that speak primarily about empowerment? Or, more practically, if she successfully becomes their friend, will they perform assigned work for her? If the Pythagorean model is the ultimate version of assumed authority—one speaking voice, no spoken dissent or critical conversation—then Helga, in moving away from that, steps onto that slippery slope of classroom authority on which many of us find ourselves lately losing our footing, especially those of us who teach in composition classrooms where the subject is race and difference.

We are increasing in numbers. Look at the rapid spread of educational multiculturalism in America.[1] Given the changing collective face of the average classroom, it should be no surprise that classroom authority is becoming more complicated. After all, one of the prerequisites—or unavoidable results—of multiculturalism is that you transform your classroom into a "contact zone," which Mary Louise Pratt now so famously defines as a space where "cultures meet, clash, and grapple with each other, often in contexts of highly asymmetrical relations of power" (34). But it seems to me that two things happen to the concept of teacher authority when the classroom becomes a contact zone. First, if the students in a multicultural classroom are grappling with their own power disparities, then how does the teacher keep the discussion productive without seeming to take sides, risking being politically marked in an explicit way that will foreclose an open exchange of ideas? And, second, how does the teacher abdicate enough authority to diminish the asymmetricality of power, but not so much that the class becomes a shapeless, directionless mass?

Contact and Conflict

The question of authority seems to me to be one of the most complex and agonistic issues of our cultural moment as composition teachers, marked as it is by the debate over how to "teach the conflicts." Yet I feel that we must be careful to understand exactly what we mean by this complicated notion of "conflict," lest we spend our time fighting the wrong fight. To Gerald Graff, for example, these "conflicts" are typically theoretical and pedagogical collisions that occur mainly behind the scenes; he would like to see "teachers in rival camps . . . engage one another in their classrooms" (12). Desiring both internal and external departmental discussions about such issues as the role of theory and canonicity, Graff would like to expose students to the "process of discussion and debate they need to see in order to become something more than passive spectators to their education" (12).

This demand for student action notwithstanding, Graff seems content with a certain level of passivity on the part of his students. He invites student response to these backstage disciplinary discussions—the "process they need to see"—but he tends to ignore, or not recognize, their participation in constructing those differences he observes. This is the other shoe that has yet to fall in the debate over teaching the conflicts. What happens to the classroom essentials we profess to believe in—heuristic learning, for example—when conflicts are taught? The power relationship in that phrase already assumes and endorses the teacher's traditional authority over the student in only a slightly more progressive version of the Pythagorean screen: "I know the conflicts; here they are." Graff disregards the extent to which students are fundamentally integral to the ways in which these conflicts have arrived in the academy and, therefore, does not understand that the students could almost certainly teach the teacher about them.

Notice that even when he realizes that he has been inattentive to his students—in his conversion narrative about his new awareness of the multiplicity of racial perspectives in *Heart of Darkness*—Graff cannot relinquish his control over those student attitudes he desires to unleash:

> I now teach *Heart of Darkness* as part of a critical debate about how to read it, which in turn is part of a larger theoretical debate about how politics and power affect the way we read literature. Without claiming to be neutral or disguising my own leanings, I try to help students adjudicate between competing arguments and make informed choices on the key points of contention. (31)

Perhaps this commentary is unfair to Graff, since he is not, after all, teaching a composition class.[2] Nonetheless, it is worthwhile to consider how his role in the classroom remains unchanged despite those social and cultural changes taking place right in front of him. In his position as traditional classroom leader shaken by the realization of African and African American perspectives on a text about imperialism, he overlooks the possibility that the black students who forced him to reevaluate his style might have more to say about oppression than evaluating competing theories. Therefore, he merely "replaces" one type of classroom control with a disguised duplicate. By keeping the discussion within the professional realm in which he holds the cards, he avoids—even shuts down—the "conflicts" he endeavors to open up.

Graff, of course, is not alone and, like Helga Crane, at least he is trying something new. We all know of teachers who have no interest at all in multiculturalism—who think it is all, as one professor recently complained to me, "so much liberal hand-wringing." These people, like the students who completely agree with them, are no doubt problematic, but they are not my concern here. My concern is with those teachers who would like to embrace the ideas of multiculturalism, but whose fears get in the way. These fears, and I freely admit to having them, are those that bell hooks describes so accurately in *Teaching to Transgress*:

> Many folks found that as they tried to respect "cultural diversity" they had to confront the limitations of their training and knowledge, as well as a possible loss of "authority." Indeed, exposing certain truths and biases often created chaos and confusion. The idea that the classroom should always be a "safe," harmonious place was challenged. It was hard for individuals to fully grasp the idea that recognition of difference might also require of us a willingness to see the classroom change, to allow for shifts in relations between students. (1994, 30)

This challenge to the "safety" of the classroom—the hard "contact" at the heart of the contact zone—is the real conflict we need to discuss, and perhaps we should not *teach* it as much as teach *with* it, *through* it, or even *against* it. What I intend to describe is similar to what hooks calls an *engaged pedagogy,* one which makes the classroom an actual site of resistance. But this resistance is, of course, both the problem and the solution. What does one do with it? How does one handle it? Even Pratt, whose article in the Modern Language Association's *Profession 91* seems to have spawned a composition subspecialty, equivocates when it comes to answering these tough questions. Her desire to interrogate "monodialectical" classroom situations concludes first with a kind of well-intentioned (and well-informed) shrug:

> Institutions have responded [to the students' need for belonging] with, among other things, rhetorics of diversity and multiculturalism whose import at this moment is up for grabs across the ideological spectrum. (39)

Our disappointment at her silence here is exacerbated by her discussion of Stanford's "Cultures, Ideas, Values" course, which, she says, operated like a contact zone of diversity. This course "put ideas and identities on the line"; in it "no one was safe" from ideological exposure (39). That is, no one was safe except for two groups: (1) those who chose to retreat to "safe houses" where people were able to "constitute themselves as horizontal, homogenous, sovereign communities with high degrees of trust, shared understanding, temporary protection from legacies of oppression" (40); and (2) teachers, whose largely unexamined presence in the classroom places something of a vertical line amidst all that horizontality. This is not to criticize Pratt; her questions about the resistance within the diverse multicultural classroom are my questions:

> What is the place of unsolicited discourse, parody, resistance, critique in the imagined classroom community? Are teachers supposed to feel that their teaching has been most successful when they have eliminated such things and unified the social world, probably in their own image? Who wins when we do that? Who loses? (39)

Frustrating those of us who want to hear her answers, however, she simply assigns the situation hypothetical status because of the increasing political impotence of faculties. However, I'm not sure that I have the answers to those questions either, yet I hope I can offer something like the beginnings of an answer. I want to examine what resistance looks like in the hands of students and teachers, and suggest that, rather than something debilitating that needs to be avoided at all costs, resistance is unavoidable and potentially productive. Therefore, we need to understand it better, to learn how to work *with* it, not in spite of it, to produce better discussions, and stronger thinkers and writers. After all, in most other pedagogical contexts, resistance is a desirable, even necessary, condition of the modern discursive classroom. Consider Kurt Spellmeyer's observation that to speak discursively is to

> enter one or more games long preceding us, games that sometimes enlarge our understanding, but also sometimes compel us to resist and renegotiate the terms of our participation. (73)

Conflict, then, is in nearly every pedagogical circumstance, one of the foundations on which we have built our house of late-century composition studies. Expressionists and constructionists alike expect their students to confront and challenge assumptions. In its more complicated form, resistance can be seen as the problem of both teachers and students. Both react to it in similar ways. Some, like Hasia Diner's student who resented having to read *The Autobiography of Malcolm X* in a "Hawthorne, Melville, and Poe" class (305) and her colleagues who agreed with him, resist openly. Others accept blindly, taking everything the teacher says as truth, even if the teacher offers the student a decentered, open-ended learning environment. Some teachers accept without question, too. They are, as Patricia Bizzell observes, "inclined to take it for granted that if the available material is pluralistic, then left-oriented or liberatory issues are bound to be addressed" (66). This is why hooks is correct in saying that multiculturalism "compels educators to recognize the narrow boundaries that have shaped the way knowledge is shared in the classroom" and "forces us all to recognize our complicity in accepting and perpetuating biases of any kind" (hooks 1994, 44). It is also why teachers and students both need to attend to the dialectical relationship between authority and resistance, and to the ways in which those "narrow boundaries" are really the inscribed cultural codes of "whiteness" that both frame that relationship and construct the default paradigm of power in the classroom.

Student Resistance: White Teachers/White Students

Most frequently, problems in classroom authority manifest themselves in methods of student resistance, and nowhere is this resistance more apparent than in the multicultural classroom where the subject is race. These strategies of contravention appear in many forms, but usually come as the result of each student's construction of a teacher with multiple meanings, texts, and subtexts. Such resistance is certainly more problematic when the teacher is a woman, a person of color, or both. As Cheryl Johnson says, "When students encounter a professor enclosed in a racial/gendered body, her very presence in the classroom inaugurates the creation of another decipherable text" (410). Students tend to decipher this text in ways that essentialize black experience; white students assume that teachers of color have a specific brand of authority over the subject of race, just as students of color are often asked to represent a typically "racial" classroom position. However, just as Johnson points out the error beneath the assumption of an ideological harmony between black professor and black student, multiculturalism becomes no less of a classroom authority problem when both the teacher and the students are, like me, white (416). Like Johnson, I am trying to understand "how my race and gender construct my role as professor, my pedagogical style, and my ideology" about the teaching of race (415).[3]

The most frequent reading students make of me, I assume, given the historical political position of most English departments (and "academics" in general) is that of the "white liberal," in the students' vague sense of that complex and loaded political terminology. Everything they hear me say is filtered through that sense of who I am and is changed in the process. This collapse of my character into the stereotyped "liberal," and the corresponding creation of a more correct "conservative," mirrors the political dichotomizing that occurs outside the classroom.[4]

The questions about teacher authority here are, of course, numerous and complex, and the implications for classroom practice are immense. What happens to a teacher's authority in a classroom that cannot construct it—cannot believe in it—in traditional ways? Let me ask this another more theoretically familiar way: What becomes of the concept of teacher authority when you intentionally place your class in a contact zone? When you demand that your students "meet, clash, grapple" with each other—and with you—and to "put ideas and identities on the line," as Pratt suggests, chances are good that the students' construction of you and your authoritative role in the classroom may suffer some erosion.

Let me clarify somewhat what I mean by this complex term *authority* before I consider the nature of one model of student resistance located in my classroom, and before I finally explore ways to continue—and refine—the process of liberatory "decentering" often typified by the work of Paulo Freire.

I say we must "refine" and even adapt Freire's ideas because his ideas of a "problem-posing" education, while extraordinarily useful as a general model of student/teacher interaction and student self-actualization, are considerably narrowed once we consider the specific relationship between the students and the teacher on which he bases his ideas. Freire the teacher seems not to have the same authority problems I have in my class; resistance is less likely when, from the very start, teacher and student agree on their asymmetrical power relationship. His students are, on the whole, aware of their oppression and powerlessness, are eager to be empowered, and clearly see him as the means to that end. Look, for example, at Freire's observations about his students' self-deprecation, their belief in his ability to change it, and their acceptance of his definition of education as the act of helping to improve their conditions:

> Not infrequently, peasants in educational projects begin to discuss a generative theme in a lively manner, then stop suddenly and say to the educator: "Excuse us, we ought to keep quiet and let you talk. You are the one who knows, we don't know anything." (45)

Gradually, however, through Freire's agency, the peasants become aware of their oppression and begin to resist *external* systems, but not the implicit system that is their educational experience. This is a demonstration of the kind of power Patricia Bizzell calls "persuasion," that which is "exercised by A over B only with B's consent, which is given only if B is convinced that doing as A suggests will serve B's best interests" (56).[5] For Bizzell, useful power is a two-stage process that she calls "authority." Dialogic at first, this process becomes less so after the student works through the persuasion stage, coming to a collaborative agreement that the teacher has expertise and has her best interests in mind. At that point, the relationship enters the second stage: the student empowers the teacher to direct the course of study without but not exclusive of any further dialogue. Freire's students eventually reach this point.

It is that early collaborative dialogue that I find compelling and useful. Unlike Graff, who seems more concerned with an assemblage of what might be called insider issues, Bizzell is interested in sharing with her students "the problematic nature of our relation as liberatory teachers to an oppressive system" (58). This is a kind of classroom authority that assumes nothing:

> The teacher cannot ask students to grant him or her authority simply on the grounds that anyone appointed to the position of teacher is thereby certified to be worthy of authority. . . . Rather, I am imagining a form of argumentation

in which the teacher demonstrates links between his or her own historical circumstances and those of the students, to suggest that their joining together in
a liberatory educational project will serve all of their best interests. (58)

This seems to me to be an ideal rendition of classroom authority. Similar
to the version offered by hooks, the equality in the classroom is complete and
thoroughgoing; the student and the teacher reveal—and learn—something
about their situated positions. If clearly articulated and enacted, this kind of
authority might have simple manifestations, such as getting work handed in on
time or having assignments read by the due date, but its more important syn-
onym is a kind of intellectual trust that the students place in their teacher. They
can clearly define their own interests as represented in the classroom, and they
know that the teacher respects and privileges these interests. Part of this self-
interest, though it might seem paradoxical, is in granting you expertise: you
know how to help them to write and think more clearly and they do not.

However, on the other hand, where matters of race are concerned, this construction of authority becomes problematic. Those resistant white students in
my class assumed a smaller gap, if any at all, between my authority and theirs.
What they feel that they have learned about African Americans from their own
experiences outweighs anything I, from my reading, or the texts from theirs,
have to tell them about oppression of blacks. Therefore, my "authority" is suspended here because the students resist and disallow that collaborative persuasion with which Bizzell begins the process. Instead, authority in this circumstance must be construed as a more elastic set of practices.

The now famous and admittedly extreme example of a teacher-authority
crisis is the case of Scott Lankford's student who wrote a disturbing essay about
a violent gay-bashing in San Francisco. The questions usually raised by this
essay, "Queers, Bums, and Magic," are all about propriety of response. Should
Lankford have considered the work fictional, criticizing its surface with little
regard to content? Or should he have assumed the events were real, and reported
the student to the police, or at least lectured the student on appropriate social
conduct? Lankford treated the essay as fiction, assigning it a low B, an approach
used to deflect the student writer's attempt to "bash" his professor. In this way,
the student "learned to cope with an openly gay instructor with some measure
of civility" (Miller 1994, 393).

Thus, the student in the contact zone of Lankford's class learns that his resistant opinions are not automatically dismissed by the teacher in ways that he
assumed, even hoped, that they would be. By heightening and then challenging
these assumptions, Lankford is able to meet with "qualified success" because
the student develops a coping strategy that serves his own interests.[6] However,
as Miller suggests, there is a third way of responding—to make the writer revise the essay from the beaten man's point of view. But even then the problem
will not go away. The student, according to Miller, will more than likely produce a work of "seamless parody," which successfully masks the student's ha-

tred under a veneer of "hyperconformity" (396). Lankford's student's essay illuminates the relationship between resistance and teacher authority because it attempts to exploit the distinction between the writer's interests and those of the teacher.

This type of student resistance is at the far end of the spectrum of responses found within the classroom contact zone; at the other end are what we might call "the converted"—those students either already in accord with the principles of multiculturalism or who quickly see an opportunity to "give the teacher what he wants" by producing conformist texts. David Rothgery calls this range of response the *continuum* of possible answers, which, to him, ultimately reinforces the need for a "necessary directionality" of ethics (243). However, the majority of the classrooms I have been in are made up of those students in the middle. They don't *hate* like Lankford's student; their racism is more subtle, confused, and often self-interrogating, and their resistance poses the most insidious threat of subverting the teacher's authority.

I call this type of resistance *reconstitution* because the student reconstitutes the nature of the polarity he sees at the heart of the classroom discussion as a means to reconfigure the authority in that classroom and to make his experiences compete with the textual expressions of authors whose messages he resists. Reconstitution is, in fact, an inversion of Bizzell's notion of *authority*. First the student determines the politics of those who disagree with him in a kind of *collaborative dissuasion*. Next, he repositions himself within the framework of that opposition. As a result, in his textual presentation—though his position has not changed—it reassigns the terms of what he sees as the teacher's smugly "correct" view into a text that is at once, to use consciously simplified terms, *conservative* and *progressive*. This is not the same as "giving the teacher what he wants." It is a strategy that seeks to further the interests of both parties simultaneously. Johnson puts it this way: "Readers who encounter a racially, culturally, or linguistically different text may read their perceptions of these differences into the text, manipulating the language to conform to their culturally learned assumptions" (412).

Thus—and this is certainly not new to anyone teaching about difference—classroom discussions and writing assignments about race do not automatically change students' minds about racism. Instead, their responses tend to perform the act of "sweeping" that Miller describes; their spoken and written texts reinscribe, or reconstitute, their previously held views on race. This method of reconstitution is similar to the coping strategy of Lankford's student, but through it the student manipulates the teacher into a strategy of co-creation.

Jean: A Study in Reconstitution

As my primary example of reconstitution, I would like to talk about a student who was in an English 102 research class I taught on the topic of "Race and Rights." We read Patricia Williams' *The Alchemy of Race and Rights*, Richard

Wright's *Uncle Tom's Children,* and selections from Booker T. Washington and W. E. B. Du Bois. One day in the earliest weeks of the semester, one of the white students, I'll call her Jean, came up after class and asked belligerently, "Do we have to talk about blacks in our essays?" In a class whose stated purpose was to discuss race and rights, I explained to her, she could examine any race she chose, but since the readings were by African American writers, she might find it difficult to ignore "the problem of the color line." She was no less resistant in the next few weeks, and while she did not manifest this resistance vocally in class, I overheard a few comments that she confided to the students in her all-white peer-review group.

However, I do not wish to present Jean's work as part of a "conversion narrative," evidence that the contact zone works by making students "grapple" with things they don't understand or value and by exposing them to real-life situations that realize and resolve the problems of asymmetrical power relations. Rather, I believe that she is representative of a group of students with whom most composition teachers are familiar: white, middle class, from a homogeneous suburban or rural background, and uncomfortable talking about race. Her comments clearly indicated that she was a racist at the outset of the course; her written text suggested, on the surface at least, that she was less so by the end. But I am not convinced that she was less racist by the end of the course. Rather, I suspect that she discovered a way to act out her views on race in ways that she hoped might be interpreted as racial tolerance.

For example, in her final research project, Jean told me she wanted to write about her workplace, where she observed discriminatory work practices. When I asked her to describe these practices, she told me that there were two kinds of jobs—full-time benefits and part-time nonbenefits—and that the part-time jobs were regularly given to black candidates. The full-time, full-benefit jobs were reserved for whites. As I began to tell her how to proceed with this project, which I thought to be a classic case of racially motivated employment discrimination, she corrected me by revealing that the "discrimination" she perceived was that it was too difficult for white candidates to get any of the part-time jobs. By overlooking the restrictions against blacks and emphasizing instead white difficulty—by conflating affirmative action and reverse racism—she reconstitutes these into a "personal" definition of affirmative action that simultaneously accommodates two opposing viewpoints: one (to appeal to my interests), an outcry that discrimination is wrong, and the other (to address her own), that it is especially unfair when it affects everyone (i.e., the white middle class).

Jean's attitude here is addressed by David Roediger, who explains how the concept of reverse racism "grows out of [an] assurance among whites that they have transcended race" (14). Further, according to Roediger, white students like Jean are sure that they see the world based on merit, while "multiculturalists, affirmative-action officers, Native American fishermen, black nationalists, and pointy-headed liberals 'bring in race'" (14).

By looking at the language of Jean's essay, we can see how this reconstitution—this belief in merit—makes its appearance as her desire for a paradoxical affirmative-action policy based on the concept of earned rewards. She writes:

> At some point the employer should observe the applicant's abilities, as opposed to focusing on the expectations portrayed by the affirmative-action program. Williams believes that she became a successful law professor based on her abilities to perform her job adequately and not because of affirmative action. Although affirmative action qualified her for admission to law school, Patricia Williams would state that her true capabilities can be observed in her being a studious individual the first semester she entered college.

By glossing over the hiring issue ("at some point") and by confusing the expectations of the employer with those of affirmative action, Jean directs her focus instead onto the idea of performative accountability and aligns her interests with those of the employer. It is fine, she says, for an African American student such as Williams to be admitted to law school on the basis of her race, but after that, performance becomes the important determining factor. This reading seems in contrast to Williams' own sense of getting through Harvard Law School, "quietly driven by the false idol of white-man-within-me, and absorb[ing] much of the knowledge and values that had enslaved my foremothers" (155).

For Williams, affirmative action is a response to a complex set of sociocultural forces, leading her to this straightforward conclusion: "I strongly believe not just in programs like affirmative action, but in affirmative action as a socially and professionally pervasive concept" (121). Yet to this student, and to many other white students in that class, Williams was "unclear" about the standards issue at the heart of affirmative action and, in effect, apologetic for having taken advantage of it.[7]

I do not wish to demonize Jean, or any of my English 102 students, most of whom found themselves facing a very real cultural dilemma: talking about that which is uncomfortable in an academy that places great weight on "opening one's mind." Placed in a class with a teacher who assumed, as Henry Giroux does, that each student would show trust, sharing, and commitment to improving the quality of human life, my students saw a critical-thinking pedagogy as repressive and stifling. In their reading of my agenda, I was expecting a shocked, leftist offense at racial discrimination, and they resisted what Bizzell would call my "coercion," not by loudly articulating their opposition, but by repositioning it within the dominant terms of my discussion. Such strategies are, to Patricia Bizzell, evidence that students can be "stunningly successful at normalizing or defusing material that we might have thought was politically explosive," an activity that should not surprise us since leaving so much of the class up to the students "sends the message that what one does with politically explosive material is entirely a matter of personal choice" (66).

Yet, more than just ways of making room for their views in the class, these multivocal acts of *coping, defusing,* or *reconstituting* are, in a strange and unexpected way, *transcultural* in the broadest sense of Mary Louise Pratt's use of the term. To Pratt, transcultural texts are those where members of "subordinated or marginal groups select and invent from materials transmitted by a dominant or metropolitan culture" (36). White students, feeling isolated and threatened from their interpretation of the multicultural leaning of the classroom, cast themselves as "marginalized," as in my student's construction of herself as the victim of discrimination in her workplace.[8]

This product of a "contact zone" seems close to the intent of Pratt's original source—linguistics—where the idea of a contact language "refers to improvised languages that develop among speakers of different native languages who need to communicate with each other consistently" (1992, 6). *Contact,* in this regard, emphasizes all the things my resistant student is interested in creating: interactive, improvisational texts that assert the co-presence of separated and distinct subjects. Further, my student's writing can not only be said to be transcultural, but also a work of *anti-conquest* as well, as are all texts by people who, according to Pratt, "secure their innocence in the same moment as they assert [their] hegemony" (1992, 7).

Seen in this regard, Lankford's student produces a response that is neither anti-conquest nor transcultural in its approach because he does not identify himself as *marginalized* by the *oppressive* and dominating force of multiculturalism. Rather, he considers himself one of the majority of "right-thinking" people. His text sets its own hegemonic agenda, leaving his teacher to consider the implications. On the other hand, Jean's approach, which I believe to be the prevalent one, is subtler—more willing to make the kinds of cultural compromises that constitute what Pratt refers to as acts of self-consciously resistant *anti-conquest.* Here, again, is Jean staking out a position that simultaneously subscribes to the principles of affirmative action and attacks them as unfair:

> Affirmative action can be viewed as a political scam for whites and a conspiracy against blacks. Racism still exists in today's society through many equal-opportunity programs. Although we as a society are working towards equality between the multiple races, it is difficult to put away the past experiences of racism because our parents educate young people on their views. The views presented to the young people by their parents were in turn carried on by the generation before. Young people adopt the views and morals taught to them by their parents, which can lead to inherited racism by having preconceived ideas without getting to know the actual situation.

What does it mean for affirmative action to be at once "a political scam for whites" and a "conspiracy against blacks?" Clearly, Jean believes that as a social policy, affirmative action serves no one and is, in fact, a disservice to all. The end of this paragraph similarly shows the writer pulled in two different directions. She begins to justify the continuance of racism on grounds of a naturalized, domesticated, historical precedent, but then shifts to a realization that this "inherited racism" has, at its heart, an ignorance of the "actual situation."

Nowhere does Jean reconstitute the discussion about race into a piece of anti-conquest rhetoric more clearly than in her essay conclusion:

> As a white female, I feel that affirmative action is a positive beginning towards creating equal opportunities for everyone and diminishing racial bias within the workforce. It is important that more [African Americans] achieve top-management positions to create an atmosphere in which people can be hired on their abilities to perform, rather than their sex or race. Once there are an equal amount of "preferenced" people as white males at the top-management levels, then today's society may not need to depend upon affirmative-action programs as a means of achieving equal opportunities within the workforce.

Although her initially stated position is, at first, in favor of affirmative action, her motive for wanting to see such a program succeed is so that we can finally, and without guilt, do away with it. After aligning herself with a marginalized group—women—she appeals to a utopian future of race neutrality that Williams herself says is determined by "reference to an aesthetic of uniformity, in which difference is simply omitted" (48).

Possible Solutions: Recursive Power and Whiteness

No matter how many versions of power we consider, no matter how noble our aims in addressing the different needs of diverse student groups, questions remain. What does student resistance do to our heuristic desires? How can we work it so that self-instruction, which is based on their belief that I will look out for their interests, is not voided by their rejection of my authority? Can we solve these problems in a way that maintains our authority—their intellectual trust in us?

The first answer is that we need to conceive of authority dialectically, as a recursive power given to teachers by students, constructed of equal parts of their assent to our control of the classroom and their resistance to that control. Therefore, it is a fluid, constantly shifting process. Bizzell is right about the two-stage conception, but she errs on the side of caution by trying to fix authority into a static force. Rather, classrooms as sites of resistance operate best when the authority in them is exposed, shared, and therefore malleable.

The second answer, which is clearly related, is that we need to theorize our position in the classroom in a way that goes beyond decentering. Perhaps one way white teachers might resolve these authority dilemmas caused by resistant white students is to understand and foreground a theoretical classroom-based position of "whiteness," for both teacher and student, just as Toni Morrison, AnnLouise Keating, and others are now exploring the notion of a whiteness found in literary texts. This process is in accord with Kobena Mercer's observation that "the real challenge in the new cultural politics of difference is to make 'whiteness' visible for the first time, as a culturally constructed ethnic identity historically contingent upon the disavowal and violent denial of difference" (205–206). Such an act of exposure also reinforces Bizzell's idea of sharing with students the teacher's historical circumstances as a means of opening up liberatory possibilities.

"Whiteness," to hooks, is a "privileged signifier" (1992, 167). To Keating, whiteness is a position of "invisible omnipresence," coded with significations of domination, order, rationality, and control (905).[9] Not coincidentally, these are the same prerequisites of a teacher's traditionally defined authority—left, perhaps, as an imprint by the generations of white teachers who have laid the grid of assumed white authority over the ideal of classroom authority. As hooks observes, in Western culture, knowledge has been traditionally "shared in ways that reinscribed colonialism and domination" (1994, 30). Notice, too, that this notion of white, empowered invisibility recalls the image of Pythagoras behind his screen, unwilling (and unable) to see and encounter dissent.

Therefore, to engage in a problem-posing pedagogy is to seek to deconstruct and expose these principles of "white" power, and, in fact, such an act of deconstruction is at the heart of any attempt to decenter classroom power. The most effective way to work against a student's reconstituted resistance of my redefining of white authority is to transcend the very construct of implicit power-based authority, unveiling for all what has historically constituted the source of that authority in the first place. This does not mean that I desire to "deracialize" everyone into a bland version of "humanity," but that by foregrounding my position within a historicized idea of whiteness, I also foreground my expectations, my desires, and the very way in which I wish to construct—and even reconstruct—my definition of authority for the purposes of their self-instruction.

I am not arguing that "whiteness" is an invisible political position to these students. Certainly, Charles Gallagher is correct that this is a naive view; white students, like some of the rest of the white population at large, "are in the midst of constructing an identity and cultural space centered around a white experience" (167). That this white experience is frequently constructed as essentially nonracist gives their resistance the intonation of righteousness that underpins their acts of reconstitution. Such attitudes as "We didn't own slaves so you cannot blame us for cultural racism" and "The civil rights movement of the 1960s made everything better" may impulsively lead one to the false hope embodied by reverting to the fact-based "banking" mode, with the teacher listing the history of white hegemony to disprove these assertions. But this can only cause the student to retrench his reconstituted opposition and proclaim more assiduously that history isn't his fault.

The foregrounding of whiteness as an invisible power construct is a logical and inevitable by-product of our recent cultural discussions about identity politics. Such an activity in the classroom corresponds to all that is admirable in the goals of a problem-posing pedagogy. It decodes the white teacher's position and, therefore, creates a space to discuss the social and cultural constructions of both the concepts of race and of authority. It fulfills Kurt Spellmeyer's claim (through Foucault) that "we do not reach a common ground by reasserting what we were, but by going beyond what we are now" (210).

Student resistance is the unavoidable result of the multicultural, contact-zoned classroom, and is not necessarily a bad thing. In saying that "required self-reflexivity does not, of course, guarantee that repugnant positions will be abandoned," Miller reassures us that creating a pedagogy of the contact zone is worthwhile—that by having students "interrogate literate practices inside and outside the classroom" and by having them "work with challenging texts that speak about issues of difference from a range of perspectives," we must continue to seek to create courses that "investigate the cultural conflicts that serve to define and limit [students'] lived experience" (407).

By exposing and situating the historical similarities between the invisibility of the teacher's power and dominant—and frequently unquestioned—white power constructs, we add to the range of perspectives all our students must address, and we further their comprehension of new ways to interrogate power and authority, in and out of the classroom.

Notes

1. For a brief but insightful examination of some of the implications of multiculturalism and classroom diversity, see Hazel V. Carby's "The Multicultural Wars" in *Black Popular Culture,* edited by Gina Dent (Seattle: Bay Press, 1992).

2. In matters of teacher authority, when teaching about race, there are certainly differences between composition and literature. In fact, I would argue that the composition class is a more factious space. In a literature class, the teacher's contended authority is more often over textual representations of experience; whereas, in the composition classroom, where "content" is more undefined, the contention is frequently over the teacher's social experiences, unmediated by external texts.

3. Notice that, for the most part, I do not address the gender issue in this essay. This is for two reasons: (1) I think that in discussions about race, students tend to make more out of my being white than my being male, and (2) whatever students interpret about my whiteness is consistent with what they interpret about maleness—a position of assumed power.

4. Of course, these students are correct: I am on the political left. But the larger issue is how do my politics affect my teaching? The answer is undeniable that they do, but this effect is not to be confused with a social agenda of reform. When I teach texts about race, I seek primarily to problematize that idea for students—to get them to see the term for the social and cultural construct that it is. In short, I am not out to turn students toward the left. Rather, I am trying to perform the work of composition no less than if the text were Plato: think, and think again, about your closely held views and about the texts you read. Prejudice has no place in the college classroom because the very nature of prejudging forecloses the possibility of thought. This holds for my students who are on the left as well. I am never content to let them "think what I think." I demand the same level of questioning of them, of their use of terms, as I do of myself. For, if Cornel West is

right when he says that all Americans—of all races—believe implicitly in the idea of white supremacy, then how do I deal with whatever ideas of racialism I have within me?

5. Bizzell also details a form of power she calls *coercion,* which more closely fits the Pythagorean form I describe in the opening paragraph: "One sort of power might be imagined as exercised by A over B, regardless of B's consent or best interests. Here A uses B to benefit A, and there's nothing B can do about it" (56).

6. *Coping,* of course, is a controversial term. It is Richard Rorty's word for one of the aims of knowledge (269). It is also the concept that Spellmeyer locates in the work of Rorty and Kenneth Bruffee and finds to be ahistorical in his work *Common Ground* (see pages 193–224).

7. This lack of clarity was not due to reading-comprehension problems, but rather to a more complicated system of resistance to what such students might have seen as "the teacher's agenda," which is, to them, a subset of the larger reformation project they correctly or incorrectly think the writing program endorses.

8. See Charles A. Gallagher, "White Reconstruction in the University," *Socialist Review,* (24) 1995: 165–187.

9. A similar discussion of the essential invisible power of "whiteness" also can be found in a number of other works, including Richard Dyer, *The Matter of Images: Essays on Representations* (New York: Routledge, 1993); Michael Omi and Howard Winant, *Racial Formation in the United States from the 1960s to the 1980s* (New York: Routledge, 1993); Dana D. Nelson, *The Word in Black and White: Reading "Race" in American Literature, 1638–1867* (Oxford: Oxford University Press, 1992); David Roediger, *The Wages of Whiteness: Race and the Making of the American Working Class* (London: Verso, 1991); and Aldon L. Nielsen, *Reading Race: White American Poets and the Racial Discourse in the Twentieth Century* (Athens, GA: University of Georgia Press, 1988).

Works Cited

Bizzell, Patricia. 1991. "Power, Authority, and Critical Pedagogy." *Journal of Basic Writing.* 10: 54–70.

Bruffee, Kenneth A. 1986. "Social Construction, Language, and the Authority of Language: A Bibliographical Essay," *College English* 48: 773–790.

Diner, Hasia R. 1993. "Some Problems with 'Multiculturalism'; or, 'The Best Laid Plans . . .'" *American Quarterly.* 45 (2): 301–308.

Freire, Paulo. 1994. *Pedagogy of the Oppressed.* Trans. Myra Bergman Ramos. New York: Continuum.

Gallagher, Charles A. 1995. "White Reconstruction in the University." *Socialist Review.* 24: 165–187.

Graff, Gerald. 1992. *Beyond the Culture Wars: How Teaching the Conflicts Can Revitalize American Education.* New York: Norton.

hooks, bell. 1992. *Black Looks: Race and Representation.* Boston: South End Press.

———. 1994. *Teaching to Transgress: Education as the Practice of Freedom.* New York: Routledge.

Johnson, Cheryl L. 1994. "The Teacher as Racial/Gendered Subject." *College English.* 56: 409–419.

Keating, AnnLouise. 1995. "Interrogating 'Whiteness,' (De)Constructing Race." *College English.* 57: 901–918.

Larsen, Nella. 1928. *Quicksand and Passing.* Ed. Deborah E. McDowell. New Brunswick, NJ: Rutgers University Press.

Mercer, Kobena. 1991. "Skin Head Sex Thing: Racial Difference and the Homoerotic Imaginary." *How Do I Look? Queer Film and Video.* Ed. Bad Object-Choices. Seattle: Bay Press. 169–210.

Miller, Richard E. 1994. "Fault Lines in the Contact Zone." *College English.* 56: 389–408.

Morrison, Toni. 1992. *Playing in the Dark: Whiteness and the Literary Imagination.* Cambridge: Harvard University Press.

Pratt, Mary Louise. 1991. "Arts of the Contact Zone." *Profession 91.* New York: Modern Language Association. 33–40.

———. 1992. *Imperial Eyes: Studies in Travel Writing and Transculturation.* New York: Routledge.

Roediger, David. 1994. *Towards the Abolition of Whiteness: Essays on Race, Politics, and Working-Class History.* London: Verso.

Rorty, Richard. 1980. *Philosophy and the Mirror of Nature.* Princeton: Princeton University Press.

Rothgery, David. 1993. "'So What Do We Do Now?' Necessary Directionality as the Writing Teacher's Response to Racist, Sexist, Homophobic Papers." *College Composition and Communication.* 44: 241–247.

Spellmeyer, Kurt. 1993. *Common Ground: Dialogue, Understanding, and the Teaching of Composition.* Englewood Cliffs, NJ: Prentice Hall.

Williams, Patricia J. 1991. *The Alchemy of Race and Rights: Diary of a Law Professor.* Cambridge: Harvard University Press.

8

Coming to Voice: "Anger Disguised and Complex, Not Anger Simple and Open"

Brad Peters

Silence and Erasure

Virginia Woolf's *A Room of One's Own* provides a compelling vignette of a woman trying to position herself among other women in history and culture. The protagonist, Mary, goes to the British Museum, where she finds womankind ubiquitously inscribed in male-authored texts. She also finds that the female is historically significant only as the object of male violence. As Mary reflects upon her discovery, she unconsciously sketches the caricature of a scholar who has written a treatise on the inferiority of women. The expression she draws on the scholar's face surprises her. It reveals "an anger disguised and complex, not an anger simple and open" (32). The reader—and not Mary—might speculate that through the sketch, she strangely projects her own anger against a masculine master narrative that constructs women as it coterminously silences them.

I juxtapose Woolf's literary figure with a front-page photograph that appeared in the campus newspaper at a university where I used to teach. The photo depicted a long line of students snake-dancing across a lawn. The caption declared that the students were celebrating diversity. All of them, male and female, were white. When an African American student visited my office, I asked her what she thought. She said she had been in the Student Union when the photographers urged everyone to march outside. She had declined to lock hands with others and join the procession. "Most of them didn't even know it was for Black History Month," she explained. "This school defines equal opportunity as a photo opportunity." The student's anecdote projects her anger against the public images and attendant rhetorics that construct a racially integrated student body by erasing non-whites.

Cinthia Gannett updates Woolf's version of the master narrative when she invokes research on male students and male teachers who disregard or appropriate women's comments in the classroom. A woman of color may not only be silenced by these practices, but also erased in classrooms where racism can deflect or render superficial our attempts at formulating discussions of "otherness." In a freshman composition classroom, for instance, I recall a young white woman who wanted to make a point about reverse racism. She nodded toward a classmate and said: "I'm not talking about Michelle. Michelle's sweet. But the blacks in my city act different. . . ."

How does an anti-racist, gender-inclusive pedagogy counteract these discursive practices so that a student might claim her voice and become visible, not as "sweet" or as an "acceptable exotic," but as a whole person? Incidents like the Black History Month photo-op and the comment about Michelle merely suggest why one African American woman—I'll call her "Tia"—wrote in her journal: "I let my emotions interfere . . . when someone says something really ignorant, I get so angry that I am unable to communicate intelligently." Tia's comment might be too easily dismissed. Sharon Welch indicates that students such as Tia are more profoundly affected than others by "the ways in which those who are in power inure themselves to the actual costs of oppression by the simple fact of shutting down, of not hearing what is said . . . when deep pain or rage is expressed" (97). bell hooks adds that these students are the ones least likely to receive support to deal with the multiple conflicts and problems they experience in an ambiance that is mostly insensitive to the cultural codes by which their own discursive practices have been shaped. It is no exaggeration to call this situation an ontological crisis.

Nevertheless, hooks points out that the speech of anger "bears witness to the primacy of resistance [and] struggle in any situation of domination," and that speaking one's anger becomes "an act of resistance, a political gesture that challenges the politics of domination that would render us nameless and voiceless" (8). It follows that if an anti-racist, gender-inclusive pedagogy is to counteract rather than replicate the structures of oppression that silence and erase the personhood of a woman of color, such a pedagogy must acknowledge her anger and open discursive spaces where she may express it. This is an early step in the deconstructive/reconstructive process that prepares a student to participate in what Welch calls an "emancipatory conversation" (98). But other steps must occur as well.

For one, teachers need to provide all students with the opportunity to establish common ground among themselves as writers and readers with tasks that they collaboratively perform. For another, students should share samples of personal writing with each other to identify their own voices and sense of position. And last, as Henry Giroux (1992) indicates, students ought to read texts that encourage them to locate their own backgrounds and life experiences within a larger social context. Accordingly, students—young women such as Tia, especially—can "move outside textuality into the world of material practices and concrete social relations" (317). In this fashion, students mutually transform each other through material interaction and become sensitized to the damaging effects of discursive practices that privilege certain *conditions of being* over others. Only so can all students discover and practice the kinds of communicative ethics that do not silence or erase those who are "other" among them. Only so can the composition classroom promote genuine, pluralistic solidarity among students when, as they participate in a multicultural curriculum, they learn about society's "patterns of systematic injustice" (Welch, 89).

I shall focus primarily on Tia's response to the pedagogical methods I've enumerated. I emphasize, however, that these methods did not, as Sandra Stotsky warns, single out Tia or any of her classmates "as token members or representatives of particular social, ethnic, religious, racial, or gender groups" (286). All students were invited to use journal-writing to explore the narrative rhetorics by which they constructed themselves and others constructed them. All students worked on assignments that had the potential of placing their narrative rhetorics in actual contact with and sometimes in resistance to others.

But this case study will examine *in particular* how Tia's journal explored the constructions of racism and whiteness, and how she felt these notions constructed her. It will trace how Tia's work incorporated counter-rhetorics that challenged those of racism and whiteness, as well as sexism, and it will indicate where those counter-rhetorics led her. It will also look at how Tia's reading resulted in an unusually insightful sense of solidarity with women writers of non-canonical texts.

My overall purpose is to suggest how such a case study might shed light on what teachers can do to accommodate the needs of women of color in a multicultural curriculum. Often as not, I fear that such a curriculum excludes the very students it is meant to support.

Narratives of Self-Recovery

Tia was the only African American woman in a group of mostly white, upper-middle-class students. She usually sat next to a white classmate, Ellen. Tia rarely chatted with Ellen or anyone else, remaining quietly observant instead. Once everyone in class began the activity of keeping a course journal, however, it was clear that Tia had plenty to say.

Tia's first journal entry briefly summarized a phone discussion with an African American friend at another university. Tia's friend had a white dorm mate who frequently used the word *nigger*—but only when she thought Tia's friend was not within hearing range. Tia went on to write:

> A similar situation happened to me two weeks ago. . . . I guess the reason I
> said nothing is that I know I would be wasting my breath. My friend Ellen . . .

and I were going to this off-campus party. . . . [T]his bar that you hang clothes on . . . kept getting in the way. . . . I ask how did she get it. . . . [S]he replies, 'my dad had to nigger-rig it.' Boy, I cannot explain my anger. . . . [S]he says things like nigger baby hair, nigger dancing, and she knows I don't like it. She says I am too racially sensitive and says I need to see a counselor. Counselor, my ass, she needs to get with it. I hate myself because I can't make her understand why it's wrong. Many white people (some of my *so-called friends*) . . . use phrases like these [emphases mine].

Although my subject position as a white male reader is problematic, I hope my interpretations will enrich, rather than hinder, alternative readings of Tia's work. For instance, I suspect that Tia saw Ellen as representative of the attitudes of her white classmates. Consequently, if Tia spoke out against racism in the classroom, whatever she said ran the risk of being discounted, or associated with psychological illness, or otherwise demeaned. Tia had little reason to expect that the classroom would become more than an extension of the world in which Ellen's and other white students' exclusive language constructed their sense of supremacy. An irony consistently permeated Tia's reference to such people as *friends*. On the other hand, Tia's journal represented a very different kind of space. Gannett's study of women's discursive practices reviews a history of how journals serve:

> . . . as a relatively safe and secret 'place' in which they might begin to escape the muting of their discourses . . . [to] harness the dialogic power . . . to inscribe themselves into the world textually, and to learn to identify and develop an array of public voices. (189)

Moreover, Tia's first journal entry showed how she shared a common psychology with women of color such as Charlotte Forten, a nineteenth-century writer, who used her journal to affirm her own potential, to vent her anger, and to resist the constructions of race and inferiority that were imposed upon her (Gannett, 140).

hooks cautions, however, that "It is possible to name one's personal experience without committing oneself to transforming or changing that experience," particularly in places of safety and secrecy such as the journal (108). Composition teachers must consider this possibility and, as Louise Wetherbee Phelps urges, reconsider journal-writing as imbricated in a series of global negotiations that young writers conduct as they determine their selfhood, their positions in society, and the meaning of their cultural backgrounds. Teachers may then approach journals as unstable texts, which, when read and responded to, become part of an on-going conversation. For instance, as Tia's reader, I felt my task was to foreground the rhetorical dynamics functioning between others' voices that she might see, such as Ellen's and her own. Such metacommentary highlights the Bakhtinian notion of *heteroglossia;* in this case, inherent ideological tensions that reside between others and Tia as she struggles to come to voice *in a context beyond the safe place of a journal.* Such metacommentary also creates what Daniel Reagan calls a "double audience" (52). If one reader in that double audience is the teacher, the other becomes the student reformulating her own experience—as Tia put it—so as to "write what I think and not what people want to hear" and "to form my own style." A young African American woman may not be able to find the support of such an audience elsewhere in a predominantly white institution.

Because of her double audience, a narrative strand emerged in Tia's journal that progressively revealed her efforts *to recover herself* from a position of silence and erasure. At one point, she wrote to recover her home culture, asking:

> When is this college thing going to improve? I feel like I'm wearing a new outfit that is really uncomfortable. . . . My mom is the one I really miss. I miss her smell and the way she kissed me before she went to work. . . . I miss collard greens, candied yams, black-eyed peas, fried okra, pot roast (without blood running out of it). I miss hearing my grandmother scoot around on her tired feet.

The equation of home culture with nourishment indicates how devoid of sustenance Tia found her new college environment. Moreover, it was the evocation of women in her family—her mother especially—that prompted Tia to start recovering key moments in her personal history as she worked toward the idea that "race" might be a constructed rather than natural category. One of the earliest moments she recalled was:

> ... when I was little, this other little girl I was in [a] line with shoved me out of the way and said, 'You're Black.' I was in total shock. My mother was not far behind me and rushed up to the girl and grabbed her arm and said, 'Of course she is, she's mine.' She put me right back in front of her.

Tia's anecdote presented a scene where the rhetoric of racism was displaced by the rhetoric of positive ethnic affirmation. As such, it established the discursive space where Tia knew she rightfully belonged as a child—even if, as a child, she needed her mother to speak in her stead. Moreover, the anecdote represents an early lesson of how a woman of color must fill such discursive space self-assertively, so as not to get "shoved out of the way" on a cultural as well as a literal level.

The agency that Tia's mother demonstrated hardly provided Tia with a lifetime model for coping. As she recounts in her journal, she encountered a fifth-grade teacher "who did not like me." The teacher's antipathy mystified her at the time. Tia wrote:

> Keep in mind I was a good student until that year. . . . I should have known when I walked up to her door and she asked me, 'Are you in my class?' and I replied yes and she replied rudely, 'Get in there then,' that I had just stepped into the depths of hell. . . . She didn't help me when I had a question or a problem. . . . I had asked for extra credit—she would give it to all the other

kids . . . but not me . . . My mother did not know what to do. She asked me if
I wanted to change classes, but I thought [this teacher] would tell all the other
teachers I was a bad student. So I stayed in hell. My mother called the principal and he . . . tried to test my intelligence with a spelling bee. . . . I felt like
he was pressing his foot on my throat. . . . Years later, I was talking to some
friends of mine who happened to be white, and they told me [this teacher] was
prejudiced. And they couldn't believe I didn't know.

Perhaps the most disturbing element in this anecdote is Tia's consistent
failure to negotiate with her teacher. Her story is not about agency, but about
the acts that suffocate it. The most significant impediment was that, at the time,
Tia could not name the racism in the teacher's and principal's pseudo-scientific
proofs or assumptions about her "deficient" intelligence. These acts did not
carry with them the rhetorical cues that accompanied the little white girl's hurtful behavior and the declaration, "You're Black!" Nor could Tia's mother intervene because no explicit act of racism could be named, exposed, or answered.
Tia recalled the teacher telling her mother: "I don't know what Tia's problem
is; she's just not a good student."

Only in her journal did Tia observe how acts of racism are not always de-
marcated by racist rhetoric. She wrote: "Because I was too little and vulnerable
[and] because she was the adult and you're always taught to respect adults, I
never stood up to that woman. . . . I learned that if you don't speak up, it can
end up damaging you." Yet Tia had no delusions about the inequities of power
that make it possible for institutionalized racism to press a foot on the throat of
a young woman of color. She added: "There are things that have happened that
I'd rather not tell . . . because even [my mother] would have said it was better
to keep your mouth shut." Tia's journal thereby became a place for confronting
the unspeakable, against which the only possibility for politicized action was
an after-the-fact dialogism that explored—or rehearsed—resistance, when her
vulnerability to immediate repercussions was no longer a worry.

An interesting twist in this episode was that Tia's white peers named the
actions of the teacher. As a result, Tia was encouraged to ponder salient responses to "The attitude I get from my white friends . . . that 'I'm white, I have
it made, sorry. It's just like that; there's nothing I can do.'" She replied, "Well,
yes, there is. They can stop using that awful word *nigger* or words like *jap* and
chink and stop telling racial jokes. They really think that's o.k." Implicitly, Tia's
observation shows that the process of self-recovery through journal-writing involves more than challenging the language that constructs white supremacy. It
also involves rehearsing confrontations with the unspeakable by moving beyond after-the-fact dialogisms to the site of everyday conversation, where she
might investigate real possibilities for present or future political action on a
personal level.

As Tia continued to write, she began to clarify for herself the importance
of establishing genuine dialogue, especially with her teachers. For example, she

reflected, "When I graduated from middle school . . . I had no trust in teachers, adults, or white people." She had encountered a number of people who, even if they "happened to be all of the above," still played an instrumental role in transforming her mistrust into trust. She went on to write about a history instructor:

> . . . he was from the cultural-friendly state of Mississippi . . . talked with a Mississippi accent . . . wore boots . . . was and still is a character. . . . Through him I learned that I was intelligent and I had potential. He restored my faith in people. . . . By the end of the year, some of the happiness I had lost during fifth grade had been restored. . . . We still keep in touch. He wrote me a letter a couple of days ago. He told me that I affected his life also. He wrote, 'Whether it be right or wrong, we are all programmed. . . . [Y]ou made me realize that my program was fouled up.' Until this letter, I never knew I had an impact on him as well.

Next, she wrote about a coach for whom, in her senior year of high school, she was a student aide:

> Now before I knew Coach, I always thought he hated Black people. During football games, he . . . makes this madman face that would send anybody running. . . . He is also known for his temper. . . . [W]hen he asked me to be his student aide, I tried to find an excuse not to do it. . . . [W]hy in the hell did he choose me? To my surprise, he turned out to be a teddy bear. . . . He has influenced my life like no other person. . . . [W]e could talk about everything. . . . Every day he would dip [tobacco], I would drink a coke, and we would talk about whatever was on our minds.

A very important thread tied these two teachers together: They both deconstructed Tia's expectations about whiteness by providing the discursive space for her to develop as a speaker. Turn-about was fair play, and she playfully deconstructed the stereotypical traits that might otherwise have marked them as potential bigots. They taught her how to speak frankly. They taught her that she had something worth saying. They taught her that communication and real negotiation of difference could happen, even between the most unlikely participants. Perhaps most interesting, the history teacher's letter suggested to Tia that the possibility exists for a woman of color to construct others in response to their construction of her. To learn that this kind of agency is possible even with white male teachers evidently caused Tia to see that racism is "mutually constitutive and socially produced" (Gates, 309).

Tia's journal thus defines self-recovery as an intellectual activity that involves potential for developing voice through several kinds of resistance. *Symbolic* resistance occurred in her response to the mundane and institutional situations that might have eclipsed her cultural background or feminine role models. *Dialogical* resistance occurred in Tia's response to the unspeakable, as her anti-racist language chipped away the patina of racist language. *Sustained* resistance occurred as she replicated an intersubjective conversation with academic voices that had advocated, accompanied, and encouraged her own, so that she might carry that conversation forward at an unfamiliar school with me, her reader.

An overview of Tia's process of self-recovery also suggests that composition teachers need to keep at least two thoughts in mind if they are seriously committed to an anti-racist pedagogy. First, a young woman of color may most readily resist the rhetorics of white supremacy *by practicing the subjective.* An anti-racist pedagogue, therefore, must be wary of theories that preclude or discourage subjectivity in writing. Second, composition instructors may be the only ones—regardless of our frequently problematic subject positions—to offer a young woman of color the opportunity to develop a voice that not only articulates her own subjectivity, but also helps her to realize the possibilities of intersubjectivity. hooks warns that many such students continue to encounter institutionalized racism and sexism that seek to humiliate them, terrorize them, or break their spirits, so that they may not otherwise envision intersubjective alliances at all (58).

The discussion that occurs between student and teacher is hardly the sole means by which a woman of color begins to write and speak intersubjectively. Other kinds of discussion must occur as well. The following pages describe Tia's forays into the public life of the classroom.

"I Am an Integrated Person"

Even before Tia began her journal, she questioned constructions of race—and gender. In an assignment on an incident that tested her communication skills, Tia recalled a confrontation in a fast-food restaurant. She and two white friends had gone there following a Tina Turner concert. She wrote:

> . . . the guys that worked there kept trying to 'hit' on us. . . . And just because I did not respond to one of them, he retorts, 'Oh, so you one of them *white girls.* . . .' I've had to deal with other people of my race calling me that for too long. . . . So I said, 'Oh, so you know how Black people are supposed to act.' He says, 'Yeah, I'm from Lincoln High School and it's all Black. . . .' I said, 'What does that have to do with me? Just because I act different than what you're used to, I'm a *white girl.* Baby, you don't know a thing about me.' . . . The other guys thought it would be best if I left, and at that point I did, too. . . . [S]omeone would have really gotten hurt, and I am not so sure it would have been me. He was still yelling immature little comments like, 'I got pictures of girls that look much better than you. . . .'

I shall not speculate how a Tina Turner concert might have affected this lively exchange. And again, I am wary of how my subject position affects my reading. But what seems to have angered Tia most was the construction the young man put on her as a "race traitor" because she did not respond to his overtures. Tia's retorts in turn demonstrate what I shall call a *counter-rhetoric,* which actively challenged and began to deconstruct the young man's categories of race and gender. At the end, she tried to make her point about blackness— and refuted his attempt to construct her as white. As a result, the young man could only attack her on the criterion that was fundamental to his construction of women: their looks. Tia's counter-rhetoric cast aspersions on a criterion for the construction of men: their physical strength. This exchange contested a number of boundaries, once more finishing in Tia's resistance to "race" as a commonly agreed-upon category. She explained:

> It really disturbs me when Blacks categorize other Blacks just because they may have a number of white friends, or they happen to dress, act, or talk different than what they're used to. Attitudes like that separate and stereotype us as a people. We should embrace characteristics that are different. . . .

Tia would repeatedly imply that characteristic differences such as class, education, accent, family background, social image, dress, and friendly relations with whites had led others to construct her as "white." Thus, her confrontation with the African American man represented only one instance of a much more complex struggle in her personal and ethnic identity. But Tia's reflection indicates that counter-rhetoric serves a conciliatory rather than a divisive purpose. Even if it ostensibly confronts someone, its ongoing process is stipulative, collaborative, acculturative, and ultimately epistemic—culminating in the paradoxical notion of "embracing difference." Counter-rhetoric is rooted deeply in volatile conversational exchanges where the speaker might not always articulate what she wants to say, and can only do so upon reflection. Counter-rhetoric is a tool for critical thinking.

In her journal, Tia wrote much more about relationships between men and women, asserting that "Some people view me as somewhat of a male-basher, and I guess I am to a certain extent. But . . . it's not because of the few bad relationships I've had." She was currently dating a white man she'd met in high school. She valued his gentle treatment of her. The boyfriend's mother was another issue. In one entry, she wrote:

> A friend and I were talking about my relationship with my boyfriend . . . It seems she overheard . . . that his mother was in church every day praying we would break up. Oh Lord, have mercy on her, that's as obscene as me asking God to castrate all the men. . . . My friend tries to help me understand this woman's racism [as] . . . the way she was raised. . . . Parents should worry about the quality of the person their son or daughter is dating, not the color. . . . We all bleed red.

Here, Tia's counter-rhetoric re-created a speaking situation that answered the rhetorics of racism and sexism by mimicking their form. She countered the prayer of her boyfriend's mother with a prayer of her own, which deconstructed what the mother had purportedly said. Tia then deconstructed her friend's apologia for her boyfriend's mother, refuting the idea that people must remain bound by historio-familial constructions of racism. Her counter-rhetoric also identified what the dominant rhetoric tried to erase: racism and so-called interracial dating. Rather than effect a conciliation that was based on acculturation, Tia thus formulated an argument for changing cultural behaviors based on what she felt should be universally anti-racist, familial ethics. This argument destabilizes the assumption of her boyfriend's mother: that God endorses "racial purity."

Probably because of her confidence in this argument, Tia did something unexpected when I assigned every student to prepare a journal entry for class-wide sharing. Despite the option of writing a new entry for the occasion, Tia chose to share the story of her boyfriend's mother. Accordingly, Tia's textual voice entered the domain of the classroom. Many students read and wrote comments on Tia's entry. They centered on her generalizations about parents and red-bloodedness. Only one note of discord sounded. A young man felt her mock-prayer exemplified "her male-bashing attitude." Otherwise, Tia had mapped out a ground of common assent about race and gender on which she inscribed her voice.

In another situation, a young white woman in her geology lab urged her to join a sorority. When Tia replied that there were only three black people in the entire white Greek system, her labmate answered: "You're not black, though. You're white." Tia wrote in her journal:

> White people have this awful habit of characterizing 'Black' as . . . a person with no manners. . . . When they see or meet a Black person who does not fit America's stereotype, they tend to say . . . : 'You're different, you're not Black, we don't consider you Black, you don't act Black.' Well, if I'm not Black, what is? . . . Black is not something you *try* to be, it is what you are. You can't act Black. You can act ignorant, but you can't act Black. Why would I want to belong to something as racially segregated as a sorority? . . . I am an integrated person. I like to be around integrated people, whether it be in church, school, at a restaurant, or a movie theater.

The counter-rhetoric in this passage revealed a far more powerful technique than resorting to essentialisms as a basis for conciliation. Once Tia examined the rhetoric of whitewashing, she supplanted it with an ontological definition that did not cave in to the "white supremist assumption" that integration means abandoning African American identity for a white one (hooks 67). Tia's construction of blackness as a non-choice and integration as a true choice also resonates with Paulo Freire's assertion that "The integrated person is person as Subject. In contrast, the adaptive person is person as object, adaptation representing at most a weak form of self-defense" (hooks 67).

Equipped with clearly delineated concepts of blackness and integration, Tia was ready to take the next step and publicly critique the more subtle nuances of racist rhetoric. She did so when the class moved on to an activity that accompanied reading the first few chapters in Mary Crow Dog's *Lakota Woman*. The activity grew out of the persistent theme of white racism that Crow Dog experiences. The students had to interview someone not about racism, but about the more general problem of discrimination. They had to summarize their interviews, analyze their reactions, and share their findings in class with small groups. They would then determine if their evidence pointed to increasing or diminishing attitudes of cultural tolerance, or if discriminatory patterns had reached a stasis.

Tia interviewed "an old high-school teacher and friend," who recalled getting turned down for a job. He complained of gender discrimination because a woman was hired. Tia's counter-rhetoric emerged *in the classroom* as she reported:

> [My former teacher] believed the way to resist discrimination was to judge a person on his or her performance and ability. When he told me this, I simply replied, 'Don't you believe man brought it upon himself?' He replied, 'I cannot argue with that statement. . . .' I always hear people complaining about Affirmative Action being reverse discrimination. . . . People do not seem to realize if there had been no discrimination against . . . women and Afro-Americans, Affirmative Action would not exist. And even though the person applying for the job may not personally be responsible for injustices done to others, he or she will have to pay the price for other people's ignorance. . . . [D]iscrimination only hurts everyone.

Here, Tia combined women's concerns and race concerns. She used the assignment to establish the interview as the site of confrontation. In the discursive space of the classroom, this counter-rhetorical position enabled her to speak non-confrontationally, without imposing a sense of "white guilt" on white students. Her analysis evolved from *her former teacher's concession* that white males brought affirmative action on themselves. Coupling the cause of women with that of African Americans compelled the white women in Tia's group to identify with her perspective, at least in part. Tia's call to resist discrimination ended with characteristic humor, as she asserted, "If you do not face it, it will keep multiplying and get worse, kind of like a roach problem." Rather than disintegrating into inter-group hostility or "privileging victimhood," the discussion stayed focused on how discrimination self-perpetuates (Stotsky 285–86). Tia cited Mary Crow Dog's aphorism, "Racism breeds racism in reverse" (34). Accordingly, Tia demonstrated to her peers how "the lives of . . . various groups are so intertwined that each is accountable to the other" (Welch 95).

The movement of Tia's counter-rhetorics—from her confrontation with the African American man to her small-group discussion of affirmative action —illustrates Bakhtin's observation that "the chain of speech communication . . . cannot be broken off from the preceding links that determine it . . . giving rise within it to unmediated responsive reactions and dialogic reverberations" (94). Through the series of assignments, Tia came to voice in the classroom because she saw the potential of counter-rhetorics to crack the hermetic seal on closed systems of thinking. Instead of merely writing, then speaking, from a perspective as the marginalized "other," Tia thus began to use counter-rhetorics as a way to shuttle between the margins and the center. She began to see that solidarity was possible not only with a trusted teacher-as-reader, but with many groups whose views, convictions, prejudices, sympathies, or antipathies might shift, depending on what became their central concern—whether it be white privilege, male privilege, African American male privilege, white female privilege, or other. In turn, marginality itself became for her what Gates identifies, tongue-in-cheek, as "the privileged site of cultural critique" (315).

Composition teachers must provide opportunities for all students to experiment with counter-rhetorics in as many ways as we can invent, without placing an onus on women of color to risk isolating themselves as "other" when they voice their perspectives or stories. With that caveat in mind, I shift from confrontation and counter-rhetorics to noncanonical texts, among whose voices, perspectives, and stories women of color can situate their own. Tia's experiences with these texts will take up the remaining discussion.

Constructing Solidarity

Even if the noncanonical text has more recently become evident in composition classrooms, Susan Gabriel has observed that school training often forces women readers—and most ironically, women of color—"to think as [white] men, to identify with a [white] male point of view, and to accept as normal and legitimate a [white] male system of values" (129). The phenomena of *immasculation* and *inculturation*, therefore, may lead students and teachers alike to subvert a noncanonical text by imposing on it—even unintentionally—a model of reading that objectifies and distances women of color from the very aspects that can connect them to that text and empower them as readers. The result is that the text retains its *authority,* and the student remains outside that authority.

One of my goals in Tia's class was to encourage students to move in degrees from the objective model, as Gabriel defines it, to a subjective one and then, ideally, to an intersubjective one. Before we read Crow Dog's *Lakota Woman,* we worked with a cross-cultural reader, Verberg's *Ourselves Among Others,* which I felt would facilitate this progression. With candor, Tia wrote: "One helpful aspect was being able to choose our own selections . . . [but] the times I really loathe writing are when I have to relate to an assigned story. To me, that is like having to churn fresh butter."

Tia implied that a young woman of color may not find studying the literature of other cultures any easier than studying that of a white-dominant one. In Tia's first reader-response paper, entitled "Coming of Age," she tried hard to find a subjective connection to "Nisa's Marriage," a story about a Botsowanan woman whose "family threatened her into accepting marriage rather than approaching her in a more loving way" (Shostak 272–79). She decided to compare the story to her family's pressure on her to get baptized—which she experienced when "I was too old for it . . . [and] came to the conclusion that God would just have to accept me without it." Tia's reading elided several issues that were unsettling from a woman's perspective: Nisa's being treated as property; Nisa's father threatening to beat her if she does not stay with the man to whom she's been given; Nisa's terror and pain as she experiences marital rape; Nisa's betrayal by a female friend and her mother when she runs off and hides. Instead, Tia focused on issues more often associated with male character-identification: autonomy, abstract moral development, formal rights and rules, denial of affective relations—all contextualized in an individualistic and hierarchical framework of thinking (Flynn, 115–16). After summarizing the story briefly and recounting her baptism at length, Tia wrote: "I discovered [baptism] was not that bad, just like Nisa discovered . . . that being married was not a great discomfort. . . . [P]eople can only say so much to influence you, but it is you who has to make the choices concerning your life."

Patrocinio Schweickart cautions that when a student is first invited to interpret a text from a subjective position, that student may engage herself in "denying the existence of a meaning authorized by the text" and resort to "the unequivocal definition of reading as . . . *only* the re-creation of [her] identity theme" (1990, 80, 90). In a written reflection, Tia verified as much, adding that she only "read to find the information I needed to write the paper."

In the second paper—one that Tia wrote about "The Idea of Family"—she demonstrated more comfort and success in reading subjectively. She summarized Gyanranjan's "Our Side of the Fence and Theirs" in more detail, saying:

> This story was about a family who . . . always considered the family next door to be strange. For instance . . . , the [narrator] is disturbed at the fact that his neighbors are always laughing . . . [and] that the daughter of the family allows her shawl to fall off and expose her bosom when she is overcome with laughter. . . . He stresses that they should have beaten her. The difference between the two families is [that] one believes in a strict value system, while the other has a more relaxed system. My family is a combination of both of these families. My dad believes girls should be home at 9 PM, not date until they're twenty-one, or go over to a boy's house. My mom attempts to be liberal. . . .

Tia's personal narrative demonstrated a much greater sensitivity to reading as "an occasion for self-recreation and expression, and as part of the process of cultivating, nurturing, and elaborating one's identity," without eliding one of the more salient issues the text raises: differences in the strictness of codes regulating the behavior of women (Schweickart 1990, 82). Tia did not seriously question these differences but was content just to point them out, perhaps because she was concentrating more on sharpening her skills of analogous thinking. In this sense, "the text is not a mere object, like a stone, but the objectification of a subject" (83). At the same time, a weak intersubjective element resides in Tia's comparison of her father's strictness and her mother's liberality to the two families in the text. She did not develop it, possibly because she was as uneasy about analyzing the codes of behavior for an East Indian family as she was about analyzing an African woman's reaction to an arranged marriage.

On the other hand, Tia pursued the possibility for intersubjective connections more consciously as she continued to read about women's issues. In a third essay, written on "Women and Men," she read Francine du Plessix Gray's "Sex Roles in the Soviet Union" and observed:

> Men in the Soviet Union tend to be passive, irresponsible, and lacking in gentlemanly qualities. . . . Therefore, Soviet women undertake the major burdens of society as well as family. Soviet women and American women share something in common. Both cultures of women do the majority of household duties, work, and take care of the children. But unlike American women, they are more respected . . . and are considered the driving force in a typical family as well as in their society. . . .
>
> When I was a senior, we had a female principal. Now before she came, our school was very violent and relaxed in its rules. Upon her arrival, our school improved. I had always thought it was interesting how one little woman, no taller than five feet, could accomplish what male principals had been trying to accomplish for years. Of course, men are not willing to give her the credit she deserves.

At this moment in her developing subjectivity, Tia acquired the sense of "oppositional criticism," which Robert Con Davis describes as the deliberate choice to resist the narratives of the dominant culture in favor of ones that provide different perspectives and possibilities of change. Concurrently, Tia's oppositional criticism created a basis for solidarity among women from different cultures. This was something that she'd been unable to establish as successfully in her preceding reader responses. As such, her critique suggested an unfolding awareness of a "dual perspective" in which she remained mindful that her reading was informed not only by her own experiences, but by other women's drives, apprehensions of personal and social history, conditions, and experience (Schweikart 1990, 92). The emergence of a dual perspective accordingly indicates a student's move toward intersubjectivity.

I hoped that such a preparation would eventually help all students to form intersubjective connections with Crow Dog's *Lakota Woman.* As a Native American activist in the American Indian Movement, Crow Dog and her world seemed far removed from theirs. But Tia formed an unusually early intersubjective connection through an in-class response to Crow Dog's opening chapters. She wrote:

> The passage on pg. 4 . . . discusses the savage deaths of [Crow Dog's] friends, the mistreatment of her sister-in-law, her years in Catholic school, her rape. The most important line of the entire passage is when she says, 'If you plan to be born, make sure you are born white and male.' Here, to me, she demonstrates how America really is, and not just on an Indian reservation. . . . I can also identify . . . I feel the same way.

There was far more at work here than identity politics or incipient separatism. Tia brought the feminist solidarity she'd constructed from her other readings together with Crow Dog's issues of white racism and aligned them with her own issues, which she'd explored primarily in her journal. She had begun to see that:

> Feminist readings of female texts are motivated by the need 'to connect,' to recuperate, or to formulate . . . the context, the tradition, that would link women writers to one another, to women readers and critics, and to the larger community of women. (Schweickart 1986, 48)

Tia's sense of solidarity with "the larger community of women" became even more apparent when the class went on a library search for a source that reflected mainstream America's image of Native American culture. They had to share their written-up findings in small-group discussion. Tia chose an article that emphasized the problem of alcohol abuse among Indians. She resisted this image, saying:

> I have often heard people talk about Indians . . . as poverty-stricken, overweight alcoholics. However . . . I listened to a speech a girl gave last year [in my high school]. A point she made was that if you were given nothing but government meat and cheese all your life, you would be fat, too. Her speech gave me more insight into the injustices that are done to . . . a proud group who fell victim to the selfishness of others . . . as well as [to] society's stereotypes.

At this stage, Tia's oppositional criticism emphasized—perhaps even celebrated—the persistence and survival of a group of people in spite of the range of formidable forces that threatened them (Schweickart 1986, 51). The group was not a woman's culture, yet the solidarity that Tia had already formulated between herself and a community of women writers seemed to encourage her to call up the text of her former classmate's pro-Indian speech. She thereby critiqued the academic article to her current classmates, whose reading of *Lakota Woman* she felt the article alone could not sufficiently illuminate. In orchestrating the interaction among these texts, Tia made great strides toward understanding the complex intersubjectivity among different women writers and speakers—even while she focused most concretely on the dynamics between racism and classism.

Next, in an assignment designed to encourage intertextual associations between *Lakota Woman* and essays from *Ourselves Among Others,* Tia wrote:

> . . . Mary Crow Dog describes her first encounter with racism as a young child. Mary explains: 'I made friends with a little white girl. She said, "Come to my house."' Mary's grandmother had warned her not to visit white people's homes, but she decided to go anyway. She writes: 'Suddenly I heard the door banging . . . it was the little girl's mother and she was yelling, "You open this door! You got some nerve coming into my home"' (23). The mother chased Mary all the way home with a whip. This incident makes one realize the in-

nocence of a child and the ignorance of an adult. In "The Stolen Party," . . . a
little girl named Rosaura . . . is deceived when she is asked to attend a birthday party . . . [by] the daughter of her mother's employer. . . . [Rosaura] at-
tends the birthday party and helps serve [refreshments]. . . . She is shocked
when . . . the employer gives her money . . . This occurrence of *class racism*
is not as violent as Mary's, but it is just as disturbing [emphasis mine]. Because Mary was an Indian, she was treated like an animal, whereas Rosaura
was treated differently simply because she was in a different class.

When Tia brought these texts together, she illustrated an understanding of
Giroux's assertion that the construction of race is never "merely about people
of color," because power configurations and social practices occurring among
various "ethnic, social, and gender locations" complicate that construction im-
measurably (1991, 249). Tia's attempt to connect the two texts became evident
when she coined the term *class racism*. Immediately thereafter, she differen-
tiated constructions of race and class while still recognizing the principles of
domination and oppression at work in both. Tia also touched on a more subtle
theme—how adults in each story separated female children who might otherwise transgress the practices of racism and classism to form a new generation's
more egalitarian community of women. Tia did not explore this second theme,
but her increased alertness to the notion of solidarity—and to the potential of
solidarity to disrupt the principles of domination and oppression—emerged in
the consequent assignment.

The culminating project for the semester was an essay that identified a
topic in *Lakota Woman* and developed it, using outside sources that went beyond a more restrictive analysis of the book alone. One of Tia's first, most surprising intersubjective connections expanded on a point she had made earlier.
It involved the incident where Mary is chased from the little white girl's house.
In a draft, Tia wrote:

> The little white girl's mother chased Mary home with a whip. This experience
> is what began her hatred of White people at a young age. I have had similar
> experiences, though not as violent. I can remember having this White friend
> as a little girl. Her mother would never allow her to come over to my house or
> for me to go over to her house. . . . I was too young to see what was happen-
> ing until one day she asked me to go shopping. I was so excited. I put on my
> new outfit and curled my hair. She called me and said they would be there soon.
> Soon turned into never. The next day at nursery school, I asked her about it
> and she ignored me. . . . The contrast between my experiences with racism and
> Mary's is that mine was less violent, as well as a psychological racism. The
> type of incidents I have experienced may not give you a black eye or busted
> ribs, but they hurt just as much. . . . My Black friends have this habit of say-
> ing White people can be very sly and sneaky wherever discrimination is con-
> cerned. . . . When any ethnic group practices such ignorance, it makes it hard
> to move on.

In this passage, Tia has arrived at what Schweickart calls "an intersubjective construction," where she "comes into close contact with an interiority—a power, a creativity, a suffering, a vision—that is not identical with her own," but which communicates with the representative voice of Crow Dog as another writer-of-the-self (1986, 52). The foundations of this construction are solidly anecdotal, yet its abstractions yield extremely important distinctions about racist actions, the dynamics of denial, the generational transmission of such actions, and the categorization of "White" (note the capital "W") as an ethnic group, rather than the norm by which all other groups are measured. Accordingly, Crow Dog's text not only affirmed what Tia's own economically written narrative explored, but it also compelled Tia to engage in a cultural critique articulated in a voice that at once proclaimed boldly who she was and with whom she claimed her primary solidarity.

Even so, this kind of solidarity may amount to little if it does not work beyond its own confines to engender a genuine conversation between ones who are privileged and ones who are not (Welch, 98). Tia's intersubjective construction examined this imperative directly, bringing together the cumulative wisdom of Crow Dog's experience, her own, and the commentary of another writer in the textual community. She wrote:

> Mary suffered through numerous acts of discrimination and watched her friends suffer also. I have endured my share of discrimination and have learned many coping mechanisms. The best advice I have received so far comes from the book, *The Measure of Our Success*. Mrs. Elderman writes: 'There are no easy answers to the continuing dilemmas of race in America. . . . The bottom line, however, is to believe in yourself and not let anybody—of any color—limit or define you solely by race or . . . gender. . . . Being racist and sexist are a state of mind and a choice' (25–26).
>
> Even though Mary endured many injustices inflicted by White people, she realized that all White people were not enemies. One of the ways she discovered this was in the process of trying to free her husband [from prison]. Mary began to realize that Whites and Native Americans could work together. I also had experiences where I learned to mistrust White people, but the good experiences that followed overshadowed the bad ones. . . . It is time . . . [to] devise a plan to educate. . . . America is becoming an even more diverse country. If we cannot learn to live together, we will destroy each other. . . .

With the achievement of this moment in Tia's written work, we witness the transformation toward which the project of intersubjective reading is aimed. She has selectively located herself in a dialogue that occurs well beyond the "unpublished spheres of inner speech," where Bakhtin might have relegated many of her reading responses; instead, she constructs an intertextual context that "as a whole participates and is communicated . . . and is defined by the real situation of the day" (116). Such transformative dialogue fully acknowledges that solidarity cannot be extra-ideological and cannot limit itself to a "narrow understanding of dialogism as argument, polemics, or parody" (121). For Tia, rather, solidarity articulates an ethos that reveals what Bakhtin means by "*integral* positions, integral personalities" that strengthen "through merging (but not identification), the combination of many voices (a corridor of voices) that augments understanding . . . [and] can be reduced neither to the purely logical nor to the purely thematic" (121).

For a woman of color—or any other student, for that matter—this is not the only perspective to take, but it is surely the most viable. To achieve it, she must seek and find the texts of writers who empower her to look beyond the isolation that comes from a lack of response to who she is and what she has to say. Intersubjective reading thus challenges students like Tia, as hooks says, to transform the personal into the political in ways that bring about collective as well as individual change. In other words, intersubjective reading provides the intellectual site where individual readers and writers may practice participation in *various* discourse communities, to pursue their rightful intent to be heard, and to negotiate an understanding of difference in ways that the world cannot silence or erase.

Conclusions

Giroux encourages us to envision an English classroom where the majority of the students is composed of the minority. How would noncanonical texts make an impact on these students' ability to relate to a curriculum and engage in it critically? Such texts provide all students with "forms of counter-memory" to challenge the texts of a predominantly white curriculum for an increasingly non-white American population (1992, 316–17). Patricia Bizzell imagines the entirety of English studies becoming "contact zones," where students examine "the conditions of difficulty and struggle under which literatures from different cultures come together" and then "learn to critique strategies of negotiating difference in the writing of others and to practice them in their own" (1994, 166, 169). The emphasis on *texts* is crucial here because Giroux's and Bizzell's visions of the post-secondary classroom do not yet square with the demographic reality that many teachers find among the *students* they teach.

The final year I taught at Tia's university, a colleague of mine described a discussion on racism that came up in her section of freshman composition. The one woman of color in the class mentioned how much in the minority she felt on campus. Several other students responded by asking her, "Then why don't you transfer to an all-black school?" My colleague turned the discussion back to some essays in the class text. Specific passages in these essays offered at least a modicum of support for the young woman, who might otherwise have been stifled.

As I have argued in this case study, Tia's experience occurred in a very similar class, and her experience reveals how much more must be done if young women of color are not to answer such a rhetoric of exclusion simply by disappearing. Bizzell advises that the formation of course content in composition classrooms must be collaborative, "with students drawing on their own resources in areas where [the teacher] would have great difficulty finding the material on [her] own" (1995, 603). Much of that material can come from the personal experiences students write about, the conversations they have with others, and the resources they find in contact zones outside the classroom. This approach to the multicultural curriculum, ultimately, is what enabled Tia to go beyond merely holding her own. It guided Tia and her classmates toward an intersubjective stance and the beginnings of an emancipatory conversation.

In light of what Tia learned, I am tempted to conclude this study as a success narrative. However, I cannot. Tia's writing was fraught with too many indications of how the post-secondary classroom reflects the barriers that are growing even more formidable as the current rhetoric of the Conservative Right strives to make racism and sexism the discrete fashion of the privileged in America. Whatever success Tia achieved, she and others who have participated in multicultural curricula are now confronting that conservative rhetoric and the ideology it is trying to create. The results of such a confrontation will show us teachers how well we have prepared our students to uphold the "wider struggle for democratic public life and critical citizenship" that I hope our profession affirms (Giroux 1991, 245).

Works Cited

Bakhtin, Mikhail. 1986. *Speech Genres and Other Essays.* Eds. Caryl Emerson and Michael Holquist. Trans. Vern McGee. Austin, TX: University of Texas Press.

Bizzell, Patricia. 1994. "'Contact Zones' and English Studies." *College English.* 56: 163–69.

———. 1995. "Comment and Response on "'Contact Zones' and English Studies." *College English.* 57: 599–603.

Crow Dog, Mary, with Richard Erdoes. 1990. *Lakota Woman.* New York: Harper Perennial.

Davis, Robert Con. 1990. "Woman as Oppositional Reader: Cixous on Discourse." *Gender in the Classroom: Power and Pedagogy.* Eds. Susan Gabriel and Isaiah Smithson. Urbana, IL: University of Illinois Press. 96–111.

Du Plessix Gray, Francine. 1991. "Sex Roles in the Soviet Union." *Ourselves Among Others, Second Edition.* Ed. Carol Verburg. Boston: Bedford Books. 301–08.

Elderman, Marian Wright. 1993. *The Measure of Our Success.* New York: Harper Collins Publishers.

Flynn, Elizabeth. 1990. "Composing as a Woman." *Gender in the Classroom: Power and Pedagogy.* Eds. Susan Gabriel and Isaiah Smithson. Urbana, IL: University of Illinois Press. 112–26.

Gabriel, Susan. 1990. "Gender, Reading, and Writing: Assignments, Expectations, and Responses." *Gender in the Classroom: Power and Pedagogy.* Eds. Susan Gabriel and Isaiah Smithson. Urbana, IL: University of Illinois Press. 127–39.

Gannett, Cinthia. 1992. *Gender and the Journal: Diaries and Academic Discourse.* Albany, NY: State University Press of New York.

Gates, Henry Louis, Jr. 1992. "African American Criticism." *Redrawing the Boundaries: The Transformation of English and American Studies.* Eds. Stephen Greenblatt and Giles Gunn. New York: The Modern Language Association of America. 303–19.

Giroux, Henry. 1991. "Postmodernism as Border Pedagogy: Redefining the Boundaries of Race and Ethnicity." *Postmodernism, Feminism, and Cultural Politics: Redrawing Educational Boundaries.* Ed. Henry Giroux. Albany, NY: State University of New York Press. 217–56.

———. 1992. "Textual Authority and the Role of Teachers as Public Intellectuals." *Social Issues in the English Classroom.* Eds. C. Mark Hurlbert and Samuel Totten. Urbana, IL: National Council of Teachers of English. 304–21.

Gyanranjan. 1990. "Our Side of the Fence and Theirs." *Ourselves Among Others, Second Edition.* Ed. Carol Verburg. Boston: Bedford Books. 146–53.

Heker, Liliana. 1991. "The Stolen Party." *Ourselves Among Others, Second Edition.* Ed. Carol Verburg. Boston: Bedford Books. 210–17.

hooks, bell. 1989. *Talking Back: Thinking Feminist, Thinking Black.* Boston: South End Press.

Phelps, Louise Wetherbee. 1989. "Images of Student Writing: The Deep Structure of Teacher Response." *Writing and Response: Theory, Practice, and Research.* Ed. Chris Anson. Urbana, IL: National Council of Teachers of English. 37–67.

Reagan, Daniel. 1994. "Naming Harlem: Teaching the Dynamics of Diversity." *Pedagogy in the Age of Politics: Writing and Reading (in) the Academy.* Eds. Patricia Sullivan and Donna Qualley. Urbana, IL: National Council of Teachers of English. 43–55.

Schweickart, Patrocinio. 1990. "Reading, Teaching, and the Ethic of Care." *Gender in the Classroom: Power and Pedagogy.* Eds. Susan Gabriel and Isaiah Smithson. Urbana, IL: University of Illinois Press. 78–95.

———. 1986. "Reading Ourselves: Toward a Feminist Theory of Reading." *Gender and Reading: Essays on Readers, Texts, and Contexts.* Eds. Elizabeth Flynn and Patrocinio Schweickart. Baltimore: The Johns Hopkins University Press. 31–62.

Shostak, Marjorie. 1991. "Nisa's Marriage." *Ourselves Among Others: Cross-Cultural Readings for Writers, Second Edition.* Ed. Carol Verburg. Boston: Bedford Books. 272–79.

Stotsky, Sandra. 1992. "Ethical Guidelines for Writing Assignments." *Social Issues in the English Classroom.* Eds. C. Mark Hurlbert and Samuel Totten. Urbana, IL: National Council of Teachers of English. 283–303.

Verberg, Carol. 1991. *Ourselves Among Others: Cross-Cultural Readings for Writers, Second Edition.* Boston: Bedford Books.

Welch, Sharon. 1991. "An Ethic of Solidarity and Difference." *Postmodernism, Feminism, and Cultural Politics: Redrawing Educational Boundaries.* Ed. Henry Giroux. Albany, NY: State University of New York Press. 83–99.

Woolf, Virginia. 1929, 1981. *A Room of One's Own.* New York: Harcourt Brace Jovanovich.

9

Removing Masks: Confronting Graceful Evasion and Bad Habits in a Graduate English Class [1]

Gail Y. Okawa

Knowledge emerges only through invention and re-invention, through the restless, impatient, continuing, hopeful inquiry [human beings] pursue in the world, with the world, and with each other.

Paulo Freire
Pedagogy of the Oppressed

In *Playing in the Dark,* Toni Morrison observes that "in matters of race, silence and evasion have historically ruled literary discourse" and that "the habit of ignoring race is understood to be a graceful, even generous liberal gesture" (1993, 9–10). Among graduate students in English for whom socialization to such academic cultural perspectives may become increasingly intense, such "habits" can be more entrenched. At the same time, it is not unusual that both teachers and graduate students make assumptions about a student's knowledge and experience precisely because of the nature of our roles and expectations, on the one hand, and our expectations about those roles on the other. In a graduate course designed to explore the discourses of people of color,[2] however, issues of color and race could not be left to graceful evasion or assumptions about knowledge and experience.[3] As the instructor of a course entitled "Removing Masks: Exploring American Minority Discourses" for master's-level students at a predominantly white urban university, I realized that my challenge was to redirect the averted eyes. In writing about this experience, I realize too that I not only

124

needed to "invent and re-invent" my understanding of race and racism in my teaching and learning during the class, but I also have had to reconsider several times over my own masks and discourse—my perceptions and conceptions of race and racism in my own experience—that as a teacher I bring to any class.

As I prepared my syllabus and readied myself mentally to begin this teaching experience, I searched my personal background as a third-generation Japanese American born in Hawai'i to discover the source of my own racialized language and perspectives on race and ethnicity. Being socialized in an ethnically and culturally heterogeneous city like Honolulu, I found myself relatively comfortable with ethnic and cultural difference and distinctiveness, for these topics remained forever on the surface there. As I was growing up, people in Hawai'i tended to identify and acknowledge cultural or ethnic differences readily: the Chinese girl, the "Japanee" man, the *haole* (Caucasian) tourist, the Hawai'ian teacher. Our discourse reflected an awareness of our separate, and at some points common, histories in the Islands—and our interdependency: in the post-plantation era, we lived in ethnically mixed neighborhoods, ate each other's food, often knowing and sharing each other's customs. The tensions lurked beneath those surfaces, the legacy of economic, racial, and linguistic oppression—colonialism on sugar and pineapple plantations—in an economy controlled by a white, English-speaking oligarchy.[4]

Attending graduate school in North Carolina and beginning full-time teaching in Virginia, I became aware of a very different configuration of racial relationships—a complex history of black and white people undergoing change in the wake of school desegregation—and my almost nonexistent place as an Asian American in that scheme of things. In Japan, where I studied, worked, and traveled later on, I was ethnically the same as the majority but, being an English-speaking American, was culturally and linguistically a *gaijin* (foreigner), like others who were non-Japanese. Yet another configuration.

Years later on the West Coast, working in the educational opportunity program of a large university, I associated with other ethnic groups and learned still different rubrics: Chicano, Hispanic; Native American, American Indian; Black, African American; Asian American, Asian/Pacific American—bureaucratic designations that didn't reflect the complexity of the groups, only a tacit acknowledgment of their existence, a legacy of the 1960s in the 1980s. But ethnicity was viewed frankly—sometimes with the candidness that can only come of familiarity. We spoke openly about being Black or Filipino or Tlingit or Chicano or Quinault or Asian American, learned about one another's cultural heritage, discussed the academic success and concerns of our students of color. We assumed the existence of racism as an historical, political, and social construct, though we were barely theoretical in our views, and saw our program as a means of rectifying past wrongs. In building a cross-ethnic peer tutoring program for a writing center serving ethnically diverse students, I had to explore how writing and learning issues often intersected with race, culture, and class. And more recently, working with several committees charged to deal with racial and linguistic issues in the National Council of Teachers of English and the Conference on College Composition and Communication has made sociopolitical considerations in English teaching and the profession even more salient for me.

The Path, the Plan: Rationale and Assignments

Given my personal history, I determined that the process of removing masks and confronting issues—including identity, language, race, and racism—in "minority" discourses had to be more than intellectual and metaphorical for the students. It would need to be a lived experience rather than simply a fancy postmodern title. This is Freire, whose process, as Victor Villanueva, Jr., describes in *Bootstraps:*

> . . . begins with private, lived experience. These experiences are generalized.
> In generalizing personal events, students find that nothing is value-free, that
> all is in one way or another political, is always affected by and affecting their
> conduct as citizens of the various communities they travel within and through.
> (1993, 54–55)

Especially in cross-cultural matters, those occurring in what Mary Louise Pratt (1991) has termed "contact zones," I had learned previously through my own lived experience that no one could claim omniscient knowledge of other peoples' or other groups' experiences despite the propensity of some to universalize their assumptions: ". . . teachers do not and cannot have all the answers, and we must be willing to relinquish authority, to take risks ourselves. We must start from the supposition that we are all equally ignorant and equally knowing" (Okawa 1993, 175). As much as possible, the learning in this class would be a mutual project, learning shared among the students and myself. While I would ask them to be continually reflective, I would vigilantly have to reconsider my own suppositions. Freire again. What was essential was that we all develop a bifocality of difference, seeing one's cultural self up close as well as from afar, the way others may—not an uncommon reflex among people of color. In my teaching, I was committed to an anti-racist pedagogy, to students confronting issues of race, language, class, and cultural difference directly and dialogically. Reflective thinking and writing would become critical.

Relying on this perspective and intuition in designing assignments, I developed two projects: one a research project on "masking," the other a kind of "unmasking" project. The first would ask the students to begin to examine ways in which the dominant society's discourses and practices have constructed and masked non-white minority groups like American Indians, Latinos, African Americans, and Asian/Pacific Americans in U.S. society—revealing not only the extent and nature of these constructions and distortions, but also suggesting our own complicity as individuals in maintaining them. They could choose examples reflecting their professional interests, such as publishing, literature, and education. Because we were on a ten-week quarter system, this had to be done quickly within the first three weeks, culminating in an oral presentation during Week 4, complete with a written outline or summary. No time for graceful evasion.

Their second project would involve the students exploring the discourses and theorizing of selected writers and speakers from communities of color, continuing the work we were doing in class—to gain insights into those perspectives, to glimpse how and what the writers and speakers of color see, how they would construct themselves through language. It was a project in perspectivism, what Ellen Messer-Davidow explains as a view that:

> . . . would bring together in processes of knowing the personal and cultural, subjective and objective, replacing dichotomies with a systemic understanding of how and what we see. It would explain how we affiliate culturally, acquire a self-centered perspective, experience the perspective of others, and deploy multiple perspectives in inquiry. (Ling 1987, 152)

It was an attempt to answer the question posed by my Zen master many years previous: "When you look at a flower, what do you think it sees?"

But I also wanted the students to have an avenue through which they could work out their discoveries and difficulties among themselves—not only orally but also in writing—and not monitored by the cultural protocols of a graduate classroom where the "habits" Morrison speaks of might be lingering. I recalled the dialogue journals from a graduate course that I had taken, the bonding that occurred among members of my group, how we worked through our anxieties with material that was not nearly as highly charged as the material in this course was likely to be. In shaping this activity, I asked students to do three things: (1) keep a dialogue journal, writing one entry per class according to the specifications that I outlined (i.e., use standard 8½ x 11 sheets; format or fold each page in half, leaving a wide right margin for "dialoguers"; and write a *minimum* of two half-pages per entry); (2) choose dialoguing partners in groups of two to four; and (3) write a final entry in two parts, including an overview of their writing in the journal (e.g., themes, concerns), and a comment on the role that their partners' responses played in their learning. A layering of reflections.

The readings, given the short ten-week term, could do little more than introduce students to various perspectives among writers and speakers of color and their discourse. They needed to dispel racial stereotypes and views of communities of color as monolithic entities, while providing some sense of shared racial and cultural histories and experiences in this country. Given these constraints, the texts that I finally selected included the following (in order assigned):

> "Toward a Theory of Minority Discourse: What Is to Be Done?"—Abdul R. Jan-Mohamed and David Lloyd
>
> *Lakota Woman*—Mary Crow Dog
>
> "The Two Lives"—Linda Hogan

"The Language We Know"—Simon Ortiz

"Cultural Politics in the Academic Community: Masking the Color Line"—Karla F. C. Holloway

"Atravesando Fronteras/Crossing Borders"—Gloria Anzaldúa

"Emerging Voices"—Pat Mora

Bootstraps: From an American Academic of Color—Victor Villanueva, Jr. (chapters divided among class members)

"The Forms of Things Unknown: Black Modes of Discourse"—Geneva Smitherman

Talking Back: Thinking Feminist, Thinking Black—bell hooks

Playing in the Dark: Whiteness and the Literary Imagination—Toni Morrison (chapters divided among class members)

M. Butterfly—David Henry Hwang

"I'm Here: An Asian American Woman's Response"—Amy Ling

"Masks of Woman"—Mitsuye Yamada

"Commitment from the Mirror-writing Box"—Trinh T. Minh-ha

"The New Cultural Politics of Difference"—Cornel West

The Journey: Redefining Authority and Finding Words

I had worked with graduate students on multicultural issues before, but this was my first experience teaching a graduate course. During our initial class meeting, I discovered that with the exception of a single international student from Japan, all students were visibly Euro-Americans, a very different mix from the tutors and students of color with whom I had worked in my previous position. Among the nineteen students, three were men, several were teachers in area schools, some were graduate teaching assistants, most were working on their master's degrees in English along with a professional writing and editing certificate. In many ways, I would be encountering new cultural terrain. In exploring discourses from writers and speakers of color, we were all embarking, I believed, on a journey of reflective self-location and critical cultural examination. On my syllabus, I had written "Ultimately, I hope we will come to understand the complex dimensions of such writing as Yamada's:

> My mask is control
> concealment
> endurance . . .
> Over my mask
> is your mask
> of me. . . ."[5]

Masks imposed, superimposed, and self-imposed. And I saw myself as a fellow traveler—though one who had made some previous trips; a *sensei,* one who had trodden a similar path earlier, as the Japanese word denotes—rather than an authority on what the way was. Thus, I told the class that I would serve as a resource, offering a broad perspective to work from and the opportunity—the space and time—to raise questions, to pose answers. But, I stressed, we were in the learning process *together.*

With this view in mind, on the first day of class, I set up the context for our study, suggesting the need for some "ground rules." Removing masks, with all the complexities of that metaphor among those of dominated and dominating cultures, might be a difficult process for those who were not familiar with the perspectives of writers from different American groups. So I asked that we strive to discuss highly charged issues like race, ethnicity, and difference candidly and honestly, that each student be treated with respect for his/her opinions and observations, that there be a spirit of trust, collaboration, and safety in the room. The nods indicated compliance if not willingness.

To establish a foundation for our study, we first took up a notion of rhetoric that was conceived broadly and inclusively, as Patricia Bizzell and Bruce Herzberg define it: "as a force in society and a factor in the creation of knowledge," not only "as a technique for stylistic manipulation" (1990, v–vi). Further, using this contemporary view of rhetoric as "epistemic and ideological" (vi), we would "attempt to understand the ways that self, society, and knowledge are situated in language" (vi). In this case, *self* would refer to the writers of color on the reading list, as well as members of the class.

As an initial step in this self-constructive direction, I asked students to do some autobiographical narrative writing in their journal, depicting their first encounters with people (and if not people, literature) from communities of color (e.g., African American, Latino, American Indian, Asian/Pacific American). This was an effort through narrative[6] to locate them in their own experience, to give them a relationship to and ownership of their past experiences and attitudes. For instance, Jill,[7] a first-year master's student, described a Southern childhood memory:

> I was raised in neighborhoods with no minority members, and I had little thought about this subject until I was well into high school. While I was a sophomore at Freeman High School . . . our school was "integrated" by a wee little black teenager. I admired her courage and spoke to her when I saw her in the hall (she was not in my grade), but I had no intimation of how she felt. (1-4-95)

Jill's dialogue partner admitted that she had had "a similar experience except I really didn't give much thought about minorities until *college.* My view was really limited." The sharing of experiences not only created a mutual supportiveness for the two women, but also allowed both students to reflect on their individual recollections and limitations. I had supposed that situating themselves in their personal contexts this way might allow all of the students to move toward a more conscious feeling of responsibility for their views, might give them a kind of baseline life text from which to work. As Donna Haraway asserts about *limited location* and *situated knowledge,* "in this way, we might become answerable for what we learn how to see" (1991, 190).

Ken, the lone international student, provided an outsider's experience with race relations in this country:

> Since I began studying the English language and the American culture in Japan, I . . . have had the opinion that America is the so-called "melting pot" in which people of different kinds get mixed together. . . . living and studying in the US for a while, however, I found out that my assumption is not always true. I don't deny the fact that people, regardless of race, interact with each other [in the] workplace or in school. Yet, once they finish working for the day and get home, they tend to mix only with people of the same race. . . .
>
> Until recently, I have not been sensitive about issues of race. . . . But surrounded by different racial groups, I cannot help realizing how important racial issues are to people in America, especially to people of color. Whenever I hear news concerning these kinds of problems, I feel as if [a] civil war were always going on between different groups of people in America. (1-5-95)

The comments of his dialogue partners reveal the reverberation of Ken's observations on their views of themselves:

> This is such an interesting perception! As Americans, most of us are used to such racial conflicts. Maybe we have become insensitive to the violence that is taking place—to the war. . . . (Ann)

> There [have] always been rigid racial lines drawn in America. In Youngstown, these lines are very sharp. (Joe)

Ann, a second-year master's student, is reflective as she translates and integrates Ken's perspective into her own worldview; Joe responds with informational statements, assertions that are confirming if not confessional in tone.

Concurrently, to develop a theoretical orientation for a study of nondominant cultural discourses, we began our reading with an essay by Abdul R. JanMohamed and David Lloyd, "Toward a Theory of Minority Discourse: What Is to Be Done?" In their introductory essay to the collection *The Nature and Context of Minority Discourse,* the authors posit the concept of "minority discourse" in terms of its "singularity":

> . . . the task of minority discourse, in the singular [is] to describe and define the common denominators that link various minority cultures. Cultures designated as minorities have certain shared experiences by virtue of their similar antagonistic relationship to the dominant culture, which seeks to marginalize them all. Thus bringing together these disparate voices in a common forum is not merely a polemical act; it is an attempt to prefigure practically what should already be the case: that those who, despite their marginalization, in fact constitute the majority should be able collectively to examine the nature and con-

tent of their common marginalization and to develop strategies for their re-empowerment. (1990, 1–2)

The essay both articulates and exemplifies the discourse and the concept. Ultimately, the authors explore a "positive theoretical framework," strategies for reempowerment like recognizing cultural viability, rereading transformatively, and realizing collective subjectivity (8).

This reading sent many students reeling, however, not only because of a perceived density of the discourse, but also because of what they felt was a rage so intense that they could feel it. It was for some a harsh initiation, perhaps a rude awakening, to views of which they had not previously been aware. Ann wrote extensively and candidly in her journal about her encounter with Jan-Mohamed and Lloyd's essay:

> I have just finished reading . . . "Toward a Theory of Minority Discourse". . . .
> This was our first reading assignment, and already I get the feeling this class
> will challenge me to redefine intellectual and emotional parameters. It seems
> I am entering a foreign culture of thought. The authors delve into layers I have
> not considered and therefore assumed they didn't exist. . . . Honestly, I was
> taken aback by the militant language used in this article. Dr. Okawa mentioned
> that we might feel uncomfortable with the discourse used in this class—with
> terms like *dominant society* and *master's language* and *destruction of minor-
> ity voice,* etc. I am uncomfortable with this language and more importantly
> with this ideology. It makes me shift in my seat, shuffle my feet, and wish I
> were somewhere else. This is a good sign. (1-9-95)

In class discussion, I elicited as broad a response as possible, encouraging each student to voice a reaction to the text in order to explore the full range of readings among the group. One saw the essay as a manifesto. Some were offended by it and defensive; many, like Ann, were surprised—and some were initially intimidated—by a perceived stridency of tone and diction. I was amazed by their naiveté regarding the hostility of the writers, but realized the ripeness of the moment. Encouraging them to consider the source of their surprise and offense, and indirectly to confront their racial biases and recognize the structure of racism reflected in their response, I asked if their reactions would have been the same were the writers not coming from a "minority" position. Some found themselves redirecting responsibility for their response from the authors to their own life histories, thereby acknowledging the authority of the writers themselves as authors of their own experience.

Especially during these initial class sessions, I found myself plagued by uncertainty as I observed the students struggling with the material. I questioned my choice and presentation of the readings and, to some extent, my relatively nonprescriptive pedagogy, which involved the students taking much of the lead. At one point in our discussion of JanMohamed and Lloyd's essay, a tense exchange erupted between two class members, followed by a rather awkward discussion. I was dismayed by the incident, but then intuitively saw this as the moment to play my tape of "Jumping Mouse," a tale told by Rick Williams, an Oglala Sioux storyteller, whom I had taped at a workshop that I had led with him and others several years before.[8] Concerned with listening, vision, and seeing in new ways, on multiple levels, I played it then to reinforce the concept of bifocality regarding texts as well as peer comments. The storyteller began with "Listen! There was this mouse . . ." and captured the listeners in the class as he had his original audience. Even as the minute hand inched toward 9:30 P.M. and passed quitting time, the tired students stayed. This experience not only diffused some of the tension in the room but, again, also transformed traditional definitions of authority vis-à-vis who could be seen to intervene as a symbolic mediator—in this case, the Oglala storyteller and his story. Ann responded to the experience with the following journal entry:

> I could not get to sleep after returning from class last night so I read a few more chapters in *Lakota Woman*. . . . The discussion in class yesterday disappointed me. People are not listening to each other. Strong emotions of each individual took over and each time someone spoke, they seemed to be saying, "Listen to me! This is my experience and you should learn from it . . . what I am saying is more important than what you are thinking or have said." . . . I'm hoping we can all relax a little more and allow people to think and speak without feeling the need to always respond in the negative or positive. When so many strong emotions flow . . . it's easy to become defensive. With defensiveness come[s] walls and walls hinder learning and understanding. In this class, I truly hope we can work on getting rid of our walls rather than building more than already exist. Humility is key. So is listening. (1-11-95)

Though her dialogue partners agreed with her about emotionalism, this interchange gave me the opportunity to write the following comment, providing another view as an additional responder:

> Emotions and emotionalism are not necessarily bad or negative, though this is the way they are generally perceived in academic culture. In some ways, I felt that some of what happened needed to so that people could really understand Rick's story.

Through this incident, I learned the importance of the *sensei* as guide, even at the graduate level and especially concerning controversial material. In preparing for the next class, I pursued a nagging feeling that, due to bad habits of evasion, graceful or otherwise, much had been lost or overlooked in understanding JanMohamed and Lloyd's viewpoint; that something more might be gleaned from the complexity of the previous class. I decided to present some thoughts to the group not as "the teacher" but as a participant-observer, describing what I had experienced through the class discussion. For example, I noted that our discussion seemed to shift from the authors' specific concerns and context to more generalized references to oppression and educational problems faced by "minorities," with stereotypes and generalizations becoming more prevalent in the class discourse. The effect? A diffusion of the subject, the writers' words, and their voices. I also reminded them of profound questions raised. One student had asked, "Can a white teacher have the same impact as a teacher of color? Can I really understand?" Another had responded, "How far do you want to go?" This was an important segue into a closer reading of the JanMohamed and Lloyd text, which brought the views of the writers back into focus in terms of themes and audience.

I offered other concepts that might help the class members recognize and redefine their positionality in relation to the writers of color and their discourse, to re-see, to re-orient themselves. The concept of *perspectivism* via Amy Ling and my metaphor of bifocality, both referred to previously in this essay, attempt to make the intellectual experience physical and sensory as does Ling's metaphor of "stretching [oneself] out of [one's] own skin" (1987, 153), a graphic image that seemed to strike home for a number of class members. In her essay, "I'm Here: An Asian American Woman's Response," Ling refers to such stretching as a necessary aspect of "validat[ing], respect[ing], and encourag[ing] every perspective" (153).

To provide further language for both understanding and articulation of "minority" experience and discourse, I also shared with them Pratt's discussion of auto-ethnography and transculturation. Autoethnography, being a self-constructive process, is evident when "people undertake to describe themselves in ways that engage with representations others have made of them" (1991, 35), re-presentations by the objects of domination as an act of becoming Freire's subjects. Transculturation, similarly a "phenomenon of the contact zone" (36), refers to "processes whereby members of subordinated or marginal groups select and invent from materials transmitted by a dominant . . . culture" (36). According to Pratt, "while subordinate peoples do not usually control what emanates from the dominant culture, they do determine to varying extents what gets absorbed into their own and what it gets used for" (36). Reading authors' perspectives in the context of such terms became a lesson in multicultural literacy as Karla Holloway defines it: "to learn the ways in which literacy resonates as a cultural event . . . . [where] 'reading' means educating ourselves, sometimes outside of our own cultures, so that we can appreciate the cultural expressivity and ways of representation of others" (1993, 616). We needed to develop and learn a language to do this.

The substance of the course finally began to come together as the students simultaneously encountered challenging readings, prepared their masking and unmasking projects, and dialogued in their journal.

Masking Projects

The cumulative effect of the orally presented masking projects seemed to be quite profound for many. One student called the experience "expansive." Within the scope of a few hours (five hours or two-and-a-half class periods), the

students briefly shared their individual investigations of a myriad of masks—
contortions and distortions of minority images created by pervasive dominant
cultural discourse: in children's books, advertising, broadcast journalism, film
(including animation), print journalism, art, textbooks, and educational theories. This gave them an opportunity to discover and acknowledge the collective
images of subordinated groups—evidence of the "damage" characterized by
JanMohamed and Lloyd (1990, 4)—and how these images are constructed
and layered by what Linda Hogan calls the "dominant and dominating world"
(1987, 237). It gave them a context for the autoethnographic acts of the writers. In his dialogue journal, Joe, a professional journalist, described his responses to specific presentations and then concluded, "the masking projects
opened my eyes and made me determined to keep my eyes open to incidents of
outright racism and subtle hegemony" (Entry 9). Yet, revealing conflicting
feelings rooted in persistent habits, Jill wrote:

> One thing that struck me about all of our projects, even mine: Our viewpoint
> was not objective, but judgmental. We judged our evidence and concluded that
> minorities have been/are being harmed—and we were all very verbal about
> our conclusions. I wonder if this is the right attitude for a graduate class. I won-
> der if it would be better to merely present evidence, not draw conclusions—
> at least without hearing the "other side" represented.
>
> The next question is: What other side? Hasn't the dominant culture been
> repressing, ignoring, and victimizing minorities of color ever since Colum-
> bus? How can there be another side?
>
> And yet—isn't this attitude—that there IS no "other side" to the question
> —exactly the attitude we condemn the dominant culture for having? (2-7-95)

Jill's faith in objectivity was absolutely consistent with her academic training—
although heavily critiqued by a number of the theorists we had encountered like
Haraway and Ling—so that her questions reflected a dichotomous world view
and her struggle with contrasting paradigms. In response to her points in Paragraph 2, a dialogue partner asked, "Haven't we heard the other side all along?"
And her third partner, who had not "thought about minorities until college,"
reflected on the importance of differing perspectives in her growing awareness:

> I think we accomplished something in these masking projects because we got
> away from the one view of the dominant culture and looked at things from an-
> other view. As for my own project, it has definitely changed my outlook/my
> awareness of how minorities are represented in the media and I am not talk-
> ing about that one instance but every time I pick up a magazine.

Final Projects

The most notable work among the "unmasking" projects reflected layers of
masks being explored and removed, an effort to stretch out of one's own skin
and/or one's old skin. We return to Ann, for example, who felt physical dis-ease

at the outset of the class, yet who made one of the boldest attempts to understand another's perspective—in many ways taking the greatest risk—in format, voice, possibility of appropriation. Her project "Magic Words: Into a Discourse of Listening" involved different degrees of seeing and internalizing the seeing; of moving, respectfully, from personal subjectivity through empathy to another's subjective position. Using a first-person narrative voice and view of her Lakota character Gwen Rushing River, Ann integrates story and research to explore Gwen's experience with masking and unmasking in the contact zones of her daughter's classroom, where she consents to speak on "Native American Day," choosing the story "How the Sioux Came to Be." Ann also tells of a conversation between Gwen and Jean Cormack, a white woman who seeks further understanding of Lakota traditions. At the conclusion of the story, Gwen Rushing River says:

> Now I have spoken twice without my mask. In my words there is healing and in the listening there is healing. The healing cannot happen without the listening. Neither will happen while I wear this mask. I only now recognize the mask as a product of white society, designed especially for my oppression. I don't know why I didn't see this before. I don't know why I hid behind my words rather than allowing them to empower me. One day is not enough to live with myself—*be myself*. One day is not enough to recognize nations of people. We are not extinct. We live and we will tell our story without masks. I will tell our story without masks.

> A voice I will send,
> hear me,
> the land all over
> a voice I am sending,
> hear me.
> I will live,
> I will live.

> *Sweat Lodge Song*[9]

Her *Afterword* reflects the humility and honesty with which she attempted this project and reveals much about her path:

> This is the first time I have approached a research paper from the first-person point of view. It was a rigorous exercise in stretching out of one's own skin and into another's. It was not a comfortable experience. In the early stages, I was full of trepidation about filling someone else's shoes. Who was I to speak from the perspective of another culture? Would Dr. Okawa be insulted by this approach? Am I being arrogant and presumptuous? Then I became angry. We haven't had enough time to research . . . this is an unrealistic project for the allotted time frame. This is impossible! Then it hit me. It is likely that people of color face this fear and anger every day, every class, every paper. This project put me on the outside. I was "other," and was permitted only limited access through my character, Jean Cormack. I am in no way trying to be an authority

on Native American or Lakota culture. Instead, I'm simply groping around in the dark. Once I worked through the aforementioned emotions (as well as some others), this approach seemed like the right one.

A second student, Casey, came to confront her own subjectivity as a bi-racial/bicultural individual through the course and chose to explore the discourse of her bicultural experience. Her Euro-American physical appearance had made her Pottawatomi Indian background invisible to others and to some extent to herself, making her somewhat apprehensive about taking the course in the first place. In her final journal overview, she admits:

> . . . I stepped out of my comfortably white bi-cultural closet! I did not want to do it, Gail. But I am not sorry. I am proud to be Indian, as scary as that still is for me to say. I do not speak of Indians in the past tense anymore. I realized I learned it from my mother—-it is a way of speaking without putting yourself at risk any more than necessary.

In her paper "Sacred Hoops, Sacred Vessels," Casey begins:

> My grandmother's mother was a Pottawatomi daughter who left the reservation and married an Irish-immigrant Indian trader. My grandmother's mother saw firsthand what happened to Indians in a post-Civil/Indian War America and she did not want to be Indian anymore. She wanted to know her children would live . . . (1)

In the context of the lives, she explicates her developing experience with language, discovering and rediscovering relationships, weaving prose and poetry:

> I have an Indian grandmother and an Indian mother who taught me as a child that I would naturally grow, and I would grow into the words. That I would understand them when the time for understanding came to me. In that moment, I would know.
> The duty of the child is to remember the words and the stories. They taught me as a child to listen to my conscience so God could speak to me, and I might grow wise as I grew old.
> The duty of the child is to listen and remember, remembering to respect the elders, to honor them because they came before and made your way possible. To remember that whatever you see in the stories later is what makes the stories your own medicine . . . (7)
> My mother was the one who taught me how to speak, where to find my voice. She was my first audience, so (there was reason) to speak. She taught me how to listen, not to the words, but to what was in them. It was there, she taught me, inside the words you discover what the person is really saying. Then ask if you are right. Never assume you are right. No one can speak for an-Other. That is against the code.
> Each speaks and
> all listen. (23)

My mother visually passed as white and did not directly confess her Indian heritage. Except once, when a kindness made her doubt her hesitation. The woman later called her a half-breed to the neighborhood and the children I had played with for three years called me "poor white trash" and threw garbage on our porch. We moved.

My father was visibly upset. My mother was ashamed of the trouble. I was never the same. (22)

These are the words at the center of the discourse emerging from my parents. This is the voice. Voice of the Fifth Race, suspended between two cultures seeing more than one way. (18)

Dialogue Journal Overviews

For other students, the most revealing representation of learning was in their dialogue journal entries and reflective overviews written in the last days of the class. Joe, for example, comments straightforwardly on his location as a Euro-American male grappling with different worldviews:

It's hard to write about minority discourse being part of the dominant society. I am of Czechoslovakian and English descent. My father was a World War II U.S. Army paratrooper, a schoolteacher and, to a large degree, a bigot. His views regarding minorities were dangerously narrow-minded and wrong. I was taught from an early age that the peace movement was a plot to overthrow the government, that blacks had no right asking for civil rights, and that political leaders like J. Edgar Hoover and George Wallace were the national players who made America great. . . . However, English 993 and [what] we have read have helped me come to grips with many of the Neanderthal, inane, and anachronistic viewpoints that have entrenched my cognizance since childhood.

Ken writes from his perspective as an international student about his experience with the course and journal writing:

[This course] has helped me to remove my mask. As a foreign student, I have come to America to study its culture and language. Even though I knew America consists of many different peoples, I simply thought [that] if I fully understood the dominant culture in this country, my purpose would be accomplished. Until taking this course, I have never realized the complexities of American culture and how much I ignored the cultures of color as if they did not exist at all. In this class, I could not only know about another aspect of America, but also gain new ways of looking at it.

Keeping a journal throughout the whole quarter gave me the chance to have a conversation with myself. . . . What I was trying to do in my journal more than anything else was to think and feel like the writers and the peoples of the communities that we explored. To me, this was the most powerful way to reach their minds. . . . Dialoging with [Ann] and [Joe] in the journal helped me a lot to understand more about the subject. . . . It seems to me that they tried not to be critical as I did, and that they sort of heard me out. . . . This helped a lot to build a strong communication among us. . . .

As I had hoped, Ken used this writing as a means of synthesizing and reflecting on his reading of different writers of color, formulating his own fledgling theories of "minority" discourse in the process. Caren, who writes that "the relationship of integrity and integration has played itself out as an underlying theme" in her journal entries, considers "how to integrate the truths of all that we have learned in this class and develop a way of being":

> . . . integrity/integration is a way of being and knowing. It is beyond sentiment and feeling. It is personal experience and shared experience. It is theory and the experiential testing of that theory. It is talking and listening and realizing that all truths are truths contextually and that all lies are denials of being. And while it is obvious that the dominant culture thrives on exclusion, it is not enough to know that and speak of it. Acting against the lies is the completion of that knowledge.
>
> . . . In journal discussions on Villanueva, I found that through rigorous struggle there is a way to come to terms with differences that can promote growth and understanding. Through critical consciousness, critical and cultural literacy there is a chance to disconnect ourselves [from] the old entropic cultural impositions and connect with the life force of growth—intellectual, spiritual, cultural. . . . We have to become smart, we have to become literate. Smart and literate about one another and history. . . .
>
> Now as JanMohamed and Lloyd (via Vladimir Lenin) would say, "What Is to Be Done?" I need support. I begin my subversive adventure. I want to find those gaps to crawl into and make my way.

Finally, in one of her latter entries, Casey, too, theorizes on the meaning of *minority discourse:*

> During the first week of this class, D— and I were talking about what *discourse* meant. I think it was one of the words I assumed I understood because I knew how to use it in the context of a sentence.
>
> But this class has made me stop to consider what discourse means, and what discourse theory is, beyond the academic names dropped in connection to the current thoughts about how to analyze a literary text according to whatever type of discourse mode it is defined as. Discourse theory seems to me to be related to the basic philosophy of the speaker/writer: how they define the world, what it means to be in the world, and how/who the audience is perceived by the speaker.
>
> Whenever we communicate we participate in activities of word choice to relate our perspectives. The words we choose and how we frame the information we are relaying says more about us than about how things actually are.

For instance, are we talking down because we perceive our audience to be less capable than we are? . . . . Most important, I think, is are we listening to what others have to say, considering it as equally relevant and important as what we have to say?

Traditionally, our discourse has operated in a way that gives the speaker/ writer the power, and the audience is not as significant. But what I am getting most out of the reading we are doing is the importance of concepts of community as opposed to individual personality isolated from "real life." Too much of the literature I have read from dominant-culture writers has seemed suspended somewhere outside myself. The reading we are doing here is not affecting me that way. Perhaps it is because I have more in common with oppressed populations than privileged ones and most d.c. writers are privileged.

Anyway, discourse theory to me now is expanded to include always the audience, the community sharing the event of reading. I am satisfied with that definition. It is not only what is contained in the text. It is how the text is perceived by the audience. That is an equally relevant part of the theory of discourse.

Minority discourse is rooted in community. Perhaps that is how we can overcome our dominant social alienation. (Dialogue 14)

Aftershock: A Postscript

Perhaps some members of the class walked away from the experience having completed a series of academic exercises. Several of the students, however, seem to have experienced a transformation of perspectives that was profound. More than intellectual and metaphorical, removing masks and confronting racism in language have been for them visceral, even physical, authority redefined. A number of them have chosen to continue the discussion in an informal seminar (noncredit, continuing at this writing over a year later), which we have called "Talking Across Difference: A Cross-Cultural Issues Seminar," reflecting our continued attempts to identify our positionality in society vis-à-vis language, race, and power.

As we talk, we discover how much and in what ways we may be confronting and internalizing how cultural difference has affected our ability to define ourselves and others, as well as our ability to empathize with the perspectives of groups to which we do not belong. For some, the class experience was pivotal to their growth as teachers, their heightening perceptions of their relationships with others and with their surroundings. As one student put it months after the term was over, my being in the process of discovery with them, revealing my own vulnerability, resulted in a new sense of progression, movement, and insight for some of them. My relinquishing or redefining my authority created a paradox: it allowed them more of a feeling of control regarding their own discoveries, less a feeling that they were groping hopelessly for answers that only the teacher knew. Freire, of course, anticipates this relationship. He contrasts knowledge achieved through a dynamic, organic process with the information statically deposited in students perceived as receptacles by dehumanized teachers. For Freire, dialogue and dialogical relations are the means to achieving a truly communicative, mutually humanized relationship between teacher and students.

Together with my students, I have experienced an uncertain journey as I reflect on my own naiveté and limitations in this discussion. As the tide pulls the sand from beneath my feet at the seashore, there is an unbalancing and shifting of foothold; each realization gives me a new ground from which to re-view how we create our realities and those of others. In retrospect, I realize that to begin with I had come to a rather simplistic awareness of cultural, social, economic, and political oppression within this society. Based on this awareness, I had intuitively developed an anti-racist pedagogy, but I was and am still naive in theorizing race and racism.

As I talk with my students and write, I continue to discover my own masks, hidden experiences of racism felt in my own past. In the process of this writing, I have remembered my most personalized introduction to my invisibility in the South. This occurred a few days after I had moved to Virginia for my first full-time job. I was driving back to North Carolina, a new driver in my newly purchased secondhand Volkswagen, making a trek to retrieve the last of my graduate-school possessions. The anticipated adventure escalated into much more as I wrecked my car—and myself in the process—and found myself being transported back to the town I had just left, not in an ambulance, but in a long, black hearse. Badly bruised and bleeding, I lay on a hospital gurney for two hours before being attended to by the "emergency" physician. Following my hospitalization, I was to revisit the doctor at his office where he would remove my stitches. Although the wood-frame building remains hazy in my memory, the sign on the door "Colored Waiting Room" is vividly etched there. I quickly processed the meaning of *colored* as *nonwhite* and reached for the doorknob, but was intercepted by a voice behind me: "Go in there," it said gently and, as I turned toward the man, he motioned to the door beyond, which was labeled "White Waiting Room." In some confusion, I smiled and thanked him. And he turned to open the first door.

For me today, upon reflection, this experience is formidable personal evidence that race in American society is societally and linguistically constructed myth and mythic, realized in the external and internalized colonialism that seeks to paralyze us.[10] If I am physically distinguishable from those who would be considered "white," I am hence "colored" if the choice had to be made; yet, for the most part, in that region I had no (personal, social, or economic) history and thus no value nor valuelessness. I was a nonentity, colorless. Perhaps the white doctor, who had power in the South, made a shaded choice (evidenced by my long wait on the gurney), but the black man, who had none, instantly knew that I wasn't black and defined by the same boundaries of movement as he was. Because of the "color-line" (Du Bois 1994, v *ff.*) that was deepset in Southern society, and the meaning in the words *white* and *colored,* my skin pigmentation and Asian physical features were irrelevant in the larger order of things; the doctor's power to choose and the African American man's internalized colonialism were not. After knowing "my place" in Hawai'i, I found that I had none or, at best, a dubious one, in Virginia.

Now, with others, I have learned that confronting difference and race in discourse and in life—beyond surfaces of politeness—must penetrate to our very bones. Removing masks, imposed, superimposed, self-imposed, must be a dynamic, not a static process. It ultimately must be communal. It, finally, must be useful and liberating.

Notes

1. Note: As this class evolved out of a community, so did the writing of this essay. I want to thank the "Talking Across Difference" seminar group, especially Amy A. Meyer, C. Kate Renfield, Christine Rizkallah, and Sam Vargo, for their memories and insights, and Victor Villanueva, Jr., for his unfailingly honest critique.

2. The term *people of color* is being used here, according to current practice, to refer to individuals and communities of such backgrounds as American Indian, African American, Latino/a, and Asian/Pacific American.

3. Although this was not a course concerned primarily with explicating "race" and "racism," it was aimed at understanding intersections of language, cultural identity, and experience in a rhetorical and sociopolitical context and driven by anti-racist assumptions and pedagogy. Assumptions about people of different ethnic, social, and cultural groups had to be explored and tested in this process.

4. Plantation housing in Hawai'i was originally organized according to ethnic camps, which reflected labor recruitment and immigration patterns, as well as management attempts to segregate and control the labor force. See, for example, Fuchs, Takaki, Sato, Day, and Okihiro, for historical, political, socioeconomic, and linguistic background on this period in Hawai'i's history.

5. Mitsuye Yamada. "Masks of Woman," in *Making Face, Making Soul/Haciendo Caras: Creative and Critical Perspectives by Feminists of Color,* edited by Gloria Anzaldúa, San Francisco: aunt lute books, 1990.

6. A significant body of literature exists on the importance of narrative in constructions of self and meaning in experience. See, for example, Kerby, Riessman, Rosen, and Witherell.

7. "Jill" together with "Ann" and other students' names are pseudonyms, provided for the sake of privacy and anonymity.

8. The workshop was a federally funded Training Grant in Basic Skills Session, Whitefish, Montana, April 1991.

9. Ann notes the source of this song as Richard Erdoes, *The Sun Dance People.* New York: Random House, 1972.

10. Wald (1987) defines *race* as "the social construction of racial types centering on a mythology of color, and the concommitant attempt to diminish, trivialize, displace,

and distort the culture of those groups subsumed by those mythological categories through the hegemony of a select patriarchal European aesthetic purporting to be objective" (28).

Works Cited

Anzaldúa, Gloria. 1987. "Atravesando Fronteras/Crossing Borders." *Borderlands/La Frontera: The New Mestiza.* San Francisco: aunt lute books. 1–98.

Bizzell, Patricia and Bruce Herzberg. 1990. *The Rhetorical Tradition.* Boston: Bedford Books.

Crow Dog, Mary, with Richard Erdoes. 1990. *Lakota Woman.* New York: Harper.

Day, Richard R. 1980. "The Development of Linguistic Attitudes and Preferences." *TESOL Quarterly.* 14: 27–37.

———. 1985. "The Ultimate Inequality: Linguistic Genocide." *Language of Inequality.* Eds. Nessa Wolfson and Joan Manes. New York: Mouton Publishers. 163–181.

Du Bois, W. E. B. 1994. *The Souls of Black Folk.* New York: Dover Publications. (Original work published in 1903.)

Freire, Paulo. 1970. *Pedagogy of the Oppressed.* Trans. M. B. Ramos. New York: Continuum.

Fuchs, Lawrence. 1961. *Hawaii Pono: A Social History.* New York: Harcourt, Brace & World.

Haraway, Donna J. 1991. *Simians, Cyborgs, and Women: The Reinvention of Nature.* New York: Routledge.

Hogan, Linda. 1987. "The Two Lives." *I Tell You Now.* Eds. B. Swann and A. Krupat. Lincoln: University of Nebraska Press. 231–249.

Holloway, Karla F. C. 1993. "Cultural Politics in the Academic Community: Masking the Color Line." *College English.* 55: 610–617.

hooks, bell. 1989. *Talking Back: Thinking Feminist, Thinking Black.* Boston: South End Press.

Hwang, David Henry. 1989. *M. Butterfly.* New York: Penguin.

JanMohamed, Abdul R., and David Lloyd. 1990. "Toward a Theory of Minority Discourse: What Is to Be Done?" *The Nature and Context of Minority Discourse.* Eds. Abdul JanMohamed and David Lloyd. New York: Oxford University Press. 1–16.

Kerby, A. P. 1991. *Narrative and the Self.* Bloomington: Indiana University Press.

Ling, Amy. 1987. "I'm Here: An Asian American Woman's Response." *New Literary History.* 19: 151–160.

Mora, Pat. 1993. "Emerging Voices: The Teaching of Writing." *Nepantla: Essays from the Land in the Middle.* Albuquerque: University of New Mexico Press. 143–148.

Morrison, Toni. 1993. *Playing in the Dark: Whiteness and the Literary Imagination.* New York: Vintage Books.

Okawa, Gail Y. 1993. "Redefining Authority: Multicultural Students and Tutors at the Educational Opportunity Program Writing Center at the University of Washington." *Writing Centers in Context: Twelve Case Studies.* Eds. J. Kinkead and J. Harris. Urbana, IL: National Council of Teachers of English. 166–191.

Ortiz, Simon. 1987. "The Language We Know." *I Tell You Now.* Eds. B. Swann and A. Krupat. Lincoln: University of Nebraska Press. 185–194.

Pratt, Mary Louise. 1991. "Arts of the Contact Zone." *Profession 91.* New York: Modern Language Association. 33–40.

Riessman, Catherine K. 1993. *Narrative Analysis.* Newbury Park, CA: Sage.

Rosen, Harold. 1985. *Stories and Meanings.* London: National Association for the Teaching of English.

Sato, Charlene J. 1985. "Linguistic Inequality in Hawaii: The Post-Creole Dilemma." *Language of Inequality.* Eds. Nessa Wolfson and Joan Manes. New York: Mouton Publishers. 255–272.

Smitherman, Geneva. 1977. "The Forms of Things Unknown: Black Modes of Discourse." *Talkin and Testifyin: The Language of Black America.* Boston: Houghton Mifflin. 101–166.

Takaki, Ronald. 1983. *Pau Hana: Plantation Life and Labor in Hawaii, 1835–1920.* Honolulu: University of Hawaii Press.

Trinh, T. Minh-ha. 1989. "Commitment from the Mirror-writing Box." *Woman, Native, Other: Writing Postcoloniality and Feminism.* Bloomington: Indiana University Press. 5–44.

Villanueva, Victor, Jr. 1993. *Bootstraps: From an American Academic of Color.* Urbana, IL: National Council of Teachers of English.

Wald, Alan. 1987. "Theorizing Cultural Difference: A Critique of the 'Ethnicity School.'" *MELUS.* 14: 21–31.

West, Cornel. 1990. "The New Cultural Politics of Difference." *Out There: Marginalization and Contemporary Cultures.* Eds. R. Ferguson, et al. Cambridge, MA: MIT Press. 19–36.

Williams, Richard. 1991. Storytelling of "Jumping Mouse." Training Grant in Basic Skills Workshop. Whitefish, Montana. April 1991.

Witherell, Carol. 1991. "The Self in Narrative: A Journey into Paradox." *Stories Lives Tell: Narrative and Dialogue in Education.* Eds. Carol Witherell and Nell Noddings. New York: Teachers College Press. 83–95.

Yamada, Mitsuye. 1990. "Masks of Woman." *Making Face, Making Soul.* Ed. Gloria Anzaldúa. San Francisco: aunt lute books. 114–116.

Contributors

Meta G. Carstarphen is Assistant Professor of Journalism at the University of North Texas. An experienced feature writer and investigative reporter for more than fifteen years, she was selected as one of eight 1997–1998 research fellows by the Poynter Institute for Media Studies to conduct a year-long study on how journalists are changing the way they use race in their reporting and writing.

Keith Gilyard, Professor of Writing and English, is Director of the Writing Program at Syracuse University. His books include *Voices of the Self: A Study of Language Competence* and *Let's Flip the Script: An African American Discourse on Language, Literature, and Learning.* He is currently Associate Chair of the Conference on College Composition and Communication.

Amy Goodburn is Assistant Professor of English at the University of Nebraska–Lincoln. Her research interests include critical and multicultural pedagogies, community literacy, and discourses of race and religion. She is currently writing *Reclaiming Literacies,* a study of literacy practices at the Genoa Indian School, an off-reservation federal boarding school in Genoa, Nebraska (1884–1934).

David G. Holmes is Assistant Professor of English and Director of American Studies at Pepperdine University. His current research projects include investigations of racism as intellectual discourse, the cultural literacy debate, and African American preaching during the eighteenth and nineteenth centuries.

Robert D. Murray, Jr., is Assistant Professor of English at St. Thomas Aquinas College. He is working on a book, tentatively titled *Refiguring Classroom Authority,* about the ways race and gender issues in the classroom can lead to a more complex understanding of textual authority.

Gail Y. Okawa, Assistant Professor of English at Youngstown State University, teaches and writes about multicultural literacy, cultural rhetorics, and sociolinguistics, and is especially interested in the representation and use of autobiographical narrative in such studies. She has written several book chapters and articles; she serves on the Executive Committee of the Conference on College Composition and Communication.

Brad Peters is Associate Professor and Director of Composition at California State University, Northridge. He has written articles and book chapters on writing and also writes about medieval rhetoric.

Malea Powell is Assistant Professor of English at the University of Nebraska, where she teaches American and American Indian rhetoric and literature. She currently is working on a book concerning the rhetorical practices of American Indian intellectuals over the past one hundred years. She is co-founder of the CCCC Caucus for American Indian Scholars and Scholarship.

Anissa Janine Wardi is Visiting Instructor of English and Coordinator of Cultural Studies at Chatham College, where she teaches courses in African American literature.